Narcissist Survival Guide

Taking Back Control Over a Narcissist! Understand the Narcissistic Personality Disorder, Deal with his Triggers & Manipulations, Avoid Abuse and Codependency

By

Elizabeth Broks

© **Copyright 2019 - All rights reserved.**

The content contained within this book may not be reproduced, duplicated or transmitted without direct written permission from the author or the publisher.

Under no circumstances will any blame or legal responsibility be held against the publisher, or author, for any damages, reparation, or monetary loss due to the information contained within this book. Either directly or indirectly.

Legal Notice:

This book is copyright protected. This book is only for personal use. You cannot amend, distribute, sell, use, quote or paraphrase any part, or the content within this book, without the consent of the author or publisher.

Disclaimer Notice:

Please note the information contained within this document is for educational and entertainment purposes only. All effort has been executed to present accurate, up to date, and reliable, complete information. No warranties of any kind are declared or implied. Readers acknowledge that the author is not engaging in the rendering of legal, financial, medical or professional advice. The content within this book has been derived from various sources. Please consult a licensed professional before attempting any techniques outlined in this book.

By reading this document, the reader agrees that under no circumstances is the author responsible for any losses, direct or indirect, which are incurred as a result of the use of information contained within this document, including, but not limited to, — errors, omissions, or inaccuracies.

Table of Content

Introduction 7

Chapter 1: About Narcissistic Personality Disorder 9

Signs of a Narcissist 9
    The feeling of superiority or entitlement 10
    The constant want for attention and validation 10
    Perfection 11
    The need to control 11
    Blame and deflect 12
    No boundaries 12
    Not empathetic 13
    Reasoning 14
    Split 15
    Fear 15
    Anxiety 16
    Shame 16
    Cannot be vulnerable 17

Identify Narcissistic Tendencies 17
    Can't stand criticism 18
    Suffering from low self-esteem 19
    Self-righteous and defensive behavior 19
    Cannot accept others' views 20
    They tend to project 21
    No interpersonal boundaries 22

Causes 23

Can Narcissism Factor to Something Else? 26

What Does Healthy Narcissism Look Like? 27

Severe Narcissism 30
    The understand-It-All Narcissist 31

The Grandiose Narcissist 31
The Seductive Narcissist 32
The Bullying Narcissist 33
The Vindictive Narcissist.. 34

Chapter 2: Narcissism in Different Situations... 35

Narcissistic Parents 35
Recognize...35
Set firm boundaries.. 36
Prevent yourself from being gas lighted 36
Others might not understand................................... 36

Narcissistic Partner 37

Living with the narcissist 38
Enhancement of self-esteem 38
Narcissists need sympathy 39
Incapable of seeing their true selves......................... 39

What Is Possible and What Isn't 42
Narcissists can never acknowledge their fault.......... 42
Narcissists don't apologize 43
Pick your fights 44
Narcissists are reluctant to process past fights......... 45

Set Your Boundaries and Protect Them........... 45
Narcissists have no regard for others limits 45
Verbal misuse may raise to physical maltreatment .. 48

Narcissistic Boss 49
Comprehend the source 50
React, don't respond 51
Set clear limits..51
Don't let them bother you 51
Don't encourage 52
Don't engage 52
Check everything..52

- Try not to argue 53
- Try not to be provoked 53
- Focus 53

Narcissism at Workplace 54
- Fortify your certainty 55
- Shaking your world 55
- Projection of flaws 56
- Diversion to win arguments 57
- Deprecating your opinion 57
- Extreme labeling 57
- Never appreciate 58
- Rude jokes and offensive sarcasm 59
- Cheapen your achievements 59

Chapter 3: Dealing with Narcissists 60

Manipulative Tactics Narcissists Use 60
- Denial 63
- Triangulation 64
- Pity 64
- Guilt 65
- Intimidation 65
- Hope 66
- Narcissistic Injury 67

Ways to Handle A Narcissist 68
- Understand the type 71
- Recognize your irritation 72
- Acknowledge where the conduct originates from 72
- Evaluating the context 72
- A positive outlook 73
- Don't get derailed 73
- Sense of humor 73
- The person might need help 74

Victim of Narcissistic Abuse 74

    You experience separation as a means of survival 76

You tread lightly 77

Giving up control 77

Realize 78

You self-disconnect 78
    Self-damage and self-destruct 79

Chapter 4: Regain Control 81

Get Your Life Back on Track 81
    Start your day with a bang 83
    Get lost in happiness 84

Stop an Argument with A Narcissist 94
    Try not to contend about 'right' and 'wrong' 94
    Use 'we' language 95
    Try not to anticipate an expression of remorse 95
    Get some information about a point that intrigues them 95
    Try not to take the lure yourself 96
    Make sure to put yourself first 96

Overcome Narcissistic Tendencies 97
    Stage one - acknowledge the roots of narcissism 98
    Stage two - be willing to hear other people out 98
    Stage three - put yourself in others' shoes 99
    Stage four - be mindful of your own actions 100
    Stage five - give yourself time to heal 100
    Stage six - don't wait for or expect praise 101
    Stage seven - practice kindness 102
    Stage eight - be content 103

Conclusion 105

References 106

Introduction

I want to thank you for choosing this book, "Narcissist Survival Guide - Taking back control over a Narcissist! Understand the narcissistic personality disorder, Deal with his Triggers & manipulations, avoid abuse and codependency." I hope you find the book informative in your quest to understand narcissism and the way a narcissist person can control your life.

Do you have a narcissist in your life? Do you find it difficult to deal with them? Maybe it is an overbearing boss at work? A controlling partner or parent at home? An egotistical friend who always brings you down while elevating themselves? Are you finding it difficult to deal with the overbearing, controlling, arrogant and manipulative ways of the narcissists in your life? If yes, then this is the perfect book for you.

This book is a simple guide to understanding and effectively dealing with them. Narcissists can make your life quite difficult and might often make you feel like you have little or no control in your life. Well, it is time to put an end to all this. It is time to regain control of your life and your relationships. Regardless of whether the narcissist in your life is controlling, critical, bossy, a bully, egotistical or arrogant, this book has all the answers to help you figure things out. The information provided in this book will help you understand the narcissistic personality disorder, the things that make them tick and the ways to deal with their manipulative ways.

It isn't difficult to deal with narcissists, provided you have all the information you need. When you start following a couple of simple rules, it does become easier. Once you understand the different tips and steps given in this book, you will be able to regain the control that you thought you lost.

Please don't allow the narcissist in your life control or bully you anymore! It is time to take action. It is time to empower yourself and regain control today! If you are ready to do this, then it is time for us to get started!

Chapter 1: About Narcissistic Personality Disorder

The Fifth Edition (DSM-5) of the American Psychiatric Association's Diagnostic and Statistical Manual of Mental Disorders classifies narcissistic personality disorder (NPD) as one of the ten personality disorders that are clinically recognized. NPD belongs to the category of personality disorders that are characterized by a degree of drama and emotionality that is truly extreme. There is a lot of debate about the exact definition of this disorder and there are various theories related to its etiology as well as modes of treatment.

Signs of a Narcissist

If you are trying to determine whether someone you know is a narcissist or not, then you can use a simple duck test that I use. Yes, I did call it a duck test. It is quite simple- if something seems like a duck and it quacks, then in all likelihood, it happens to be a duck. There is absolutely no need to make it complicated when it can be this simple. Unlike physical illness, you cannot use an MRI, blood test or any other test to determine narcissism. Even psychoanalysts rely on their observations of someone to determine the presence of narcissism.

There are certain behaviors and symptoms that can help you determine whether someone is a narcissist or not. An individual doesn't necessarily have to display all the traits discussed in this section and even displaying about 55% of these traits is sufficient to classify someone as a narcissist. The list discussed in this section is quite descriptive and will come in handy.

The feeling of superiority or entitlement

A narcissist's world is pretty two-dimensional- it is all about good and bad, superior and inferior and right and wrong. There is always a certain hierarchy that exists and obviously, the narcissist is at the very top. After all, that's the only place where they feel safe. Narcissists have an obsessive need to feel like they are always in control of everything, that they are the absolute best, that there is no one more competent than them and so on, I am sure you get a general idea. It is interesting to note that narcissists also get this feeling of supposes superiority by being the absolute worst- the most upset, injured, ill or wrong for a long period. Then they start to assume that they are entitled to some form of recompense and that others owe them an "apology" for their "suffering."

The constant want for attention and validation

Who doesn't like attention or validation? Everyone does and a healthy need for these things is quite normal. However, narcissists tend to constantly seek attention and validation. In fact, they will keep coming up with different ways in which they can obtain these from others to fulfill their exaggerated need for the same. Only when the validation comes from others does the narcissist feel happy. Even then, it doesn't account for much. Their need for approval is like a black hole. Regardless of all the positivity, support and praise, you give them, it will never be sufficient. This happens because a narcissist believes that no one really loves them. In spite of all their bragging, self-absorption and the sense of grandiose, all narcissists are insecure and feel like they cannot measure up. This makes them seek praise and approval from others, constantly, to stoke their fragile ego. Regardless of all that they get, they will not stop wanting more.

Perfection

Striving for perfection isn't a bad thing. However, a narcissists desire for perfection is almost obsessive. They firmly believe that they must be perfect, those around them must be perfect and that their lives must turn out exactly how they have planned and that everything needs to be perfect. It is impossible to fulfill this obsessive need for perfection and this makes the narcissists feel disappointed and miserable regardless of what they or others do. All the complaining and their dissatisfaction are due to their unreasonable demand for perfection.

The need to control

Everyone likes to be in control; being in control gives people a sense of security. Well, a narcissist's need for control is unlike that of others. A narcissist's lack of satisfaction about the way life unfolds makes them want to do everything they possibly can to control it and shape it according to their likes and dislikes. They not only want to be in control, but they also demand that they are always in control. This sense of entitlement makes them feel like the only logical option available is to ensure that they are always in control of everything. Narcissists usually have a specific storyline in mind about what everyone around them must do and say. When someone doesn't behave the way a narcissist expects, it tends to leave them feeling unsatisfied and upset. If you go off their "script," they are uncertain about what comes next and this tends to upset them. So, they start demanding that you must behave and do exactly what they say. They seem to think of you as a part of their internal storyline instead of an actual human being capable of thinking your own thoughts and experiencing feelings.

Blame and deflect

Narcissists love to be in control, but they don't like to take responsibility for anything unless it is a result that they desire. When things don't turn out the way they planned, if they feel like they are being criticized or that they aren't "perfect," then the narcissist will conveniently shift the blame onto everyone and everything around them instead of taking any responsibility for it. At times, this blame tends to be generalized- the politicians, government, the economy and so on. On other occasions, the narcissist will pick a person to blame- parents, partner, the law and so on. The narcissist will try to blame others for limiting him. Usually, the narcissist will try to blame the person that they are emotionally attached to. So, if you happen to be that person, then be prepared to shoulder a lot of unnecessary blame because the narcissist is incapable of accepting responsibility. If the narcissist accepts the responsibility when things go wrong, then their fragile façade of perfection will crack, and they try to avoid this at all costs. So, the safest option available is for the narcissist to blame you because you are emotionally attached to him.

No boundaries

A narcissist has no sense of boundaries. As I have already mentioned, for a narcissist, you are merely a character in his play. They are quite similar to children who seem to think that everything is theirs. So, the narcissist will think that you feel and experience everything the same way he does. In fact, he will be quite shocked to realize that others don't experience things the same way he does and that others can think and feel things by themselves too. If a narcissist needs something from you, then the narcissist will easily go to great lengths to get what he wants.

Not empathetic

Narcissists aren't capable of empathizing with others. They are usually self-absorbed to the extent of being selfish and are incapable of understanding what others feel. Narcissists seem to demand that others must think and feel the way that they do. Since they think like this, it isn't possible for them to empathize with others. This also means that they don't usually feel guilty, apologetic or even remorseful. However, they are certainly quite adept at spotting any perceived threat, anger or even rejection from others. Even though they can do this, they are incapable of understanding the feelings of those around them. They tend to misread facial expressions and usually have a preexisting bias and seem to think that most of the facial expressions are negative. Unless you are explicitly displaying your emotions, there's a fat chance that the narcissist will not understand them. While dealing with a narcissist, even the simplest of phrases like "I love you," or "I am sorry" can easily backfire if he is on edge. It is quite likely that he will misinterpret your comment and come back with an attack. Their inability to understand body language is a primary reason why narcissists cannot empathize with others. They cannot see, understand or even correctly interpret what others might be feeling. Apart from this, narcissists also find it difficult to understand the nature of feelings; they don't comprehend what gives rise to feelings. They usually harbor the belief that their feelings are caused by others or any other external event. They don't understand that their thoughts, interpretation of things as well as their own psychology cause their feelings. So, a narcissist will think that you caused their feelings- especially all the negative ones. They might blame you because they think that your inability to follow their plan has left them feeling vulnerable. A narcissist's lack of empathy makes it difficult for them to foster a true relationship or an emotional bond with others.

Reasoning

You might have made the common mistake of trying to use reason and logic to get a narcissist to understand the damaging effect his behavior tends to have on you. You might think that if he can understand the pain his behavior causes you, understand the hurt he inflicts, he will be able to change. This might work with an average human being; however, this will not work with a narcissist. It doesn't work because all that the narcissist is aware of are his thoughts and what he feels. Narcissists might say that they understand, but they truly don't.

This is why it isn't surprising that most of the decisions that a narcissist makes are purely based on what they feel about something or someone. If a narcissist wants a blue sports car, then their decision to make the purchase will purely be based on how they feel while driving it, instead of whether it is the right choice for them or not. If they feel bored or sad, then they will want to change things, shift, quit their job or maybe even end a relationship. They seem to think that the answer to all their problems lies in external factors. Not only do they assume this, but they also think that others must simply go along with what they do and if they don't get this, then they react in an unfavorable manner.

Split

A narcissist's personality can be split into two parts - the good and the bad. In fact, for a narcissist, the world is pretty two-dimensional. They obviously take the credit for anything good that happens and conveniently blame others for all the things that go wrong. They don't pay any heed to the consequences of their negative words or deeds and instead accuse others of being critical. Not just that, narcissists often remember things as either good or bad, wonderful or terrible and so on. They can only deal with one perspective and that's theirs. They cannot remember the good and the bad aspects of a situation; they will either remember the good or the bad and never both.

Fear

Fear seems to play a major role in a narcissist's life. Most of their fears are usually deeply buried within or suppressed. They are constantly scared of being ridiculed, rejected or even criticized by others. They might have fears about being abandoned, of being rejected by someone they life, about being attacked or even about being perceived as inadequate. All this negativity that they constantly live with makes it impossible for them to truly trust others. In fact, the closer the relationship seems to be the less will the narcissist trust you. Narcissists are scared of intimacy or vulnerability in any form. They fear that if others see their imperfections, then they will be judged, criticized or even rejected. Regardless of all the reassurances, you provide the narcissist with, they will never be able to fully trust or love anyone else. In fact, they will keep testing others constantly to find their breaking point. The unreasonable fears that they harbor prevent them from ever truly forming a bond with anyone.

Anxiety

Anxiety is a progressing inclination that something awful is either going on or is going to occur. A few narcissists demonstrate their nervousness by always talking about all the bad that will happen, while some stowaway and suppress their uneasiness. In any case, most narcissists tend to usually project any of the uneasiness, doubt or anxiety that they experience onto those they share a close bond with and tend to blame them for being unsupportive, irrational and incapable of giving the narcissist the attention he seems to think that he deserves. This is intended to transfer the anxiety to someone else so that they no longer have to experience it. The more awful and terrible that you feel, the narcissist starts to feel that much better. Truth is told he feels more grounded and increasingly in control as you feel your anxiety and misery develop.

Shame

Narcissists don't feel much shame since they think they are always right and don't think that their behavior or words will ever have an effect on anyone. Regardless of this and how they feel, they tend to harbor a great deal of shame. Shame is the conviction that there is something profoundly wrong or terrible about oneself. Stowed away in some part of the narcissist's psyche is every one of the uncertainties, fears, and rejected characteristics that he is always on the lookout for to escape from. The narcissist is intensely embarrassed about all these rejected considerations and sentiments. Keeping his vulnerabilities covered up is basic to the narcissist's imagined confidence or false self. Eventually, be that as it may, this makes it unthinkable for them to be totally genuine and straightforward.

Cannot be vulnerable

They fail to understand emotions, their lack of empathy as well as their constant need for self-assurance makes narcissists unable to cherish or even form an honest connection with others. They fail to look at the world from any other perspective except their own. They don't even seem to think that others might have any perspectives. Narcissists cannot understand all this and they are incapable of showing any vulnerabilities. They seem to think that vulnerabilities make them seem weak and this is something they cannot stand to bear.

Identify Narcissistic Tendencies

The fifth edition of the Diagnostic and Statistical Manual of Mental Disorders (DSM) lists nine different traits that can be used for determining narcissistic personality disorder (NPD). The traits described in this edition were the same as the ones that were identified over two decades ago. I believe that apart from the nine traits mentioned below, there are a couple of more traits that can be used for identifying narcissistic tendencies. These nine traits are usually displayed by anyone who can be classified, as an extreme narcissist will display all these traits. However, the DSM is of the opinion that even if an individual only displays five of these traits, he can be labeled as a narcissist. An individual is termed as a narcissist if he displays all or at least five of these traits:

- A rather grandiose sense of their self-importance

- Is engrossed with dreams of the abundance of love, power and success. Is always preoccupied with dreams of an "idealistic" life.

- Trusts that he is truly unique and can only be understood or can bound with only those who are as extraordinary as he is.

- Requires unnecessary and constant compliments and praise.

- A deep-rooted feeling of entitlement.

- Is exploitative.

- Needs compassion but is incapable of empathizing or understanding others.

- Is usually jealous of others and trusts that it is others who are jealous of him.

- Displays haughty or egotistical mannerisms.

So, what's missing here? Well, in this section, I will provide you with information about other qualities that are missing from the list stated above. These are qualities that narcissists regularly display and have been left out from the DSM list.

Can't stand criticism

Narcissists are incredibly reactive to criticism or anything else that they perceive or interpret as a negative evaluation of their personality or overall performance. That is the reason why they either readily falsify an answer, not acknowledge something, try to change the topic or even reply like they were asked a different question altogether when they are asked a question that can make them admit any of their vulnerabilities, shortcomings or any other problems. All this goes on to show that a narcissist's ego is quite inflated. However, this ego of theirs is rather fragile and it can be punctured with the slightest of pokes.

Suffering from low self-esteem

Another aspect of the narcissist's mental makeup, which is rather interesting, is their low level of self-esteem. At least superficially, their self-esteem might appear to be better and greater assured than pretty much anyone else's. Also, given their "drive" it's not unusual for them to rise to positions of considerable power that grant them the ability to amass a fortune. However, if you study what's underneath this façade of elevated social, political, or financial stature, you will notice that there is a dearth of confidence- in themselves, their beliefs and abilities. In some ways, it almost seems like they are driven to show to themselves as well as others that the not-so-confident "inner child" present within them doesn't exist. The self-doubt that they harbor in the darkest and hard-to-reach places of their psyche is where they conveniently hide their feelings and fear of inferiority. The façade that they maintain in front of the world about their high self-esteem is nothing more than mere posturing. Their want for excessive attention does make one question where it all stems from.

Self-righteous and defensive behavior

Narcissists can be extremely self-righteous and defensive.

Their desire to shield their exaggerated, yet fragile egos makes it quite easy to activate their defense mechanisms. I've already mentioned how reactive they normally are to criticism. However, it isn't just criticism that they are sensitive to, but they are quite sensitive to anything that might challenge or question their competence. In fact, their self-preservation mechanisms will kick in even if this so-called criticism is imaginary and not real. This is why so many non-narcissists find it rather difficult to get through to a narcissist in case of an argument or a fight. For instance, in a situation that seems challenging or in the face of conflict, it seems like a narcissist's survival depends on them being right or justified. They might behave like admitting their mistake or even apologizing for the same is some form of transgression and isn't possible for them.

Also, their "my way or the highway" mindset while making decisions shows their stubborn way of thinking which betrays their underlying doubts- the fear or longing of always being right, strong, or clever. The greater is the threat (either real or imaginary, it doesn't matter) to their pretentious, privileged, exaggeratedly puffed-up self-image, the more defensive will they be.

Cannot accept others' views

Narcissists tend to react to opposing viewpoints with anger or rage. The two common emotions that a narcissist is able to express rather easily are anger and rage. In fact, most of his emotions are projected using these primitive emotions. Also, he might use the same emotions to convey all his emotions. Once they feel like they are either on the verge of feeling or reliving any difficult feelings from their past, they will try to readily project such undesirable feelings onto someone else. A narcissist finds it easier to project their feelings onto others instead of dealing with them.

The message that gets communicated via such negative feelings is "I'm not the one that's (insert a negative adjective of your choice- wrong, foolish, mistaken and so on.), but you are!" Or, it can even be something like "I'm not narcissistic or anything like that, but you are!" (Or, in a milder version it might be something like, "If I'm narcissistic or borderline narcissistic, then so are you!"). If the other individual has no clue as to what provoked their outburst, then it is quite likely that such an individual will experience some sort of confusion and even feel offended about all that was said by the narcissist. This leads me to the next point…

They tend to project

The one thing that everyone must keep in mind while dealing with narcissists is that they project their flaws onto others. So, the flaws that they are nitpicking at might not be present, but they are merely projecting their flaws onto you. Due to the fact they're compelled from somewhere deep inside to hide their shortcomings or weaknesses, so they habitually redirect any negative appraisal of themselves outwards. Narcissists seem to be of the opinion that doing so will help them keep away from their innermost suspicious about themselves. It is quite similar to cleaning a room by sweeping the dirt under the rug. So, superficially the room will seem clean, but that's not the truth. A narcissist pretty much does the same thing. By denying their true emotions about themselves, they seem to think that reality will change.

Narcissism is usually diagnosed in an individual by means

of their lack of self-insight and their falsified self-perception. One of the most reliable ways for them to feel good about themselves as well as feel "secure" with themselves is by invalidating or degrading others. They love to put others down because it makes them feel superior to others. This fake sense of grandiose makes them come across as rather cold individuals. When it comes to identifying the shortcomings of others, they will be quite perceptive. However, this heightened state of perception seems to take leave when it comes to their own shortcomings.

No interpersonal boundaries

Narcissists tend to have no idea about interpersonal space. It's been said about narcissists that they can't tell wherein they end and where the other person begins. The concept of personal space just doesn't exist in a narcissist's vocabulary. They tend to unconsciously view others as "extensions" of themselves; they regard them as existing only to serve their personal desires—just as they routinely place their desires before those of everybody else's. Narcissists seem to think of others as "narcissistic supplies" (yes, that's the word that's used in clinical literature to describe the traits of narcissists). They are of the opinion that others are present to only cater to their needs and don't think of others as independent entities with their own needs and desires. Instead, a narcissist will constantly try to think of how they might "use" others to their personal benefit. If a narcissist is trying to get something that he himself cannot provide, then they will obviously try to obtain that from others.

The lack of their perception of personal boundaries coupled with their erratically developed interpersonal abilities can also make them behave in an inappropriate manner- dominate conversations and share excessive information with others about the intimate details of their life. A narcissist might share things that an average individual might be embarrassed to share, and the narcissist will do so without an ounce of embarrassment. In fact, it might also seem like the narcissist is thriving on others discomfort. This seems to fuel the narcissist's ego too.

They can, for instance, share (that too with great pleasure) how they "chewed" someone out and think that the other person will be impressed by the narcissist's apparent display of skills, braveness or even cleverness. In reality, it is quite likely that the listener might be appalled by their lack of restraint or tact. Also, narcissists might ask others such questions which are generally considered to be too intimate or private- thereby unwittingly upsetting the other person. Such a situation might be quite challenging for someone to face, especially if the narcissist they are conversing with happens to be in a position of authority over them so that by not responding to such a question places them in jeopardy.

Well, all the additional characterizations of the pathological narcissist (along with the ones that are usually suggested as the characteristics of narcissism) can be beneficial in enabling you to identify them earlier and take the necessary precautions. If you have already been duped by a narcissist with his narcissistic and manipulative ways, then perhaps the information given in this section will give you a heads up to save yourself from any further damage.

Causes

So, what causes narcissism? Are there any specific events

that can trigger NPD? You will learn about these things in this section.

Psychologically, individuals with narcissism have a tendency of suffering from opposing ideas of their self-image. On one hand, they can have excessive admiration and a sense of grandiose about themselves, while on the other they might be constantly questioning and devaluing themselves in their minds. They may be prone to excessive emotional sensitivity.

Earlier psychoanalytic principles on the emotional traits for the development of narcissistic tendencies showed that narcissism isn't something that someone develops overnight. In fact, if observed properly, a child will start displaying the traits of narcissism and the same will be carried on him into adulthood too. It is believed that a child with narcissistic parents will display narcissistic characteristics. For instance, if the child notices that the relationship dynamics of his parents consisted of one parent doing everything possible to please the other one- and the child somehow realizes that only by pleasing the parent will he be rewarded or loved. This sort of faulty thinking will make the child believe that it is okay to hand out love only when others please you.

Further, if a child is used to receiving excessive and unrealistic admiration, reward, and overindulgence, or immoderate criticism for misbehavior at some stage in childhood, it is quite likely that the child will develop some sort of narcissistic personality disorder. There is no specific cause for narcissism, but there are certain risk factors that increase the chances of NPD and they are emotional abuse, manipulation by caregivers, lack of proper parental care and lack of interaction with others.

There aren't any exact causes that are believed to lead to a narcissistic personality disorder. However, some psychologists believe that the foundation for narcissism lies in the circumstances and activities that might have taken place during an individual's adolescence, which stimulated him in the wrong manner and lead to the development of certain narcissistic tendencies. Here are a couple of the most common reasons which experts believe might cause narcissism, but there isn't any scientific evidence that proves the same.

If the child is usually pampered by the caregivers- parents or any other individuals of the family, he might start to believe that he is extra special and that there is no one who is as perfect as he is.

Any unrealistic expectations that the parents might have from a child can create an undue strain and this, in turn, might cause the child to form similar expectations from others. Even if he doesn't enjoy it, the child might start to do everything he can to please his caregiver and meet their unrealistic expectations. So, the child starts to believe that it is okay to have unrealistic expectations and that others must fulfill the same.

Not getting enough attention from primary caregivers can make the child feel neglected and ignored. As a result, the child will start doing things in an attempt for more attention. This can be one of the reasons why a narcissist constantly demands attention from those around him- to compensate for the lack of it he received during his childhood.

In some cases, a child might grow to be a narcissist if he has faced some type of abuse like physical violence, abusive language, threatening language or anything along these lines in childhood. Their family members or the primary caregivers might have inflicted this sort of abuse upon them.

If a child is constantly told that displaying emotions is a sign of weakness and is asked to mask his feelings, then this might transform into a rather terrible trait later in life. Growing up like this will render the child from recognizing other emotions or even from understanding his own emotions. This, in turn, will make the child un-empathetic, which is one of the primary traits of a narcissist.

Can Narcissism Factor to Something Else?

In some cases, a narcissistic person might have either grown up with a narcissist or might have experienced some form of narcissism from others. As mentioned earlier, these things can trigger narcissism. For instance, a narcissistic mother or father might provide their children with various opportunities to the child to expand his horizons, but might not offer any actual motivation, support or love. A narcissistic figure might brag about their child's genius but will not do anything to aid the growth of the child. In fact, they will not even offer any guidance or assistance that might help the child in any manner.

If your partner has a narcissistic character trait, it can suggest that he probably felt deserted or unloved as a child. Additionally, your partner might have had to fight for everything that he wanted, even if they were the most basic things like love, support, and appreciation. He might have had to come up with certain defense mechanisms and build up walls around him to shield himself from all the despair and confusion he used to experience.

Narcissism is never used in a positive sense, is it? I mean, a quick Google search for narcissism will provide you with different results related to this matter like: "What is narcissism?" "How might you tell if your partner is a narcissist?" or "Am I a narcissist?" Therefore, it is not a wonder that narcissism conjures up different negative ideas in one's mind. Will you be surprised if I tell you that building positive or healthy narcissism might actually be good for you?

The idea of Narcissistic Personality Disorder is for sure exceptionally pessimistic and incorporates attributes like unhealthy levels of self-absorption, a requirement for constant adoration and an absence of compassion or empathy toward other people. Be that as it may, narcissism itself isn't certain or negative—there is a continuum from beneficial to obsessive.

What Does Healthy Narcissism Look Like?

Let us look at a hypothetical situation to gain a better understanding of what healthy narcissism looks like. Adele is a lovely, insightful and creative individual who does not perceive or welcome these characteristics in herself. One day, she mentions in passing that she never looks in the mirror. You may recollect that in the Greek legend, Narcissus was in love with his reflection. Adele isn't in love with her reflection and this turns out to be rather problematic for her. While completing a task that's difficult, she doesn't experience joy or fulfillment, but experiences a dismal feeling of "moving on to the next issue." When others comment about her style and effortless grace, she feels uncomfortable. When it comes to her personal life, she finds it surprising that someone might be interested in her or finds her attractive.

Healthy narcissism is characterized by the presence of confidence and self-esteem. It's about taking pride in one's appearance, in the way a person thinks, in the achievement of a difficult task that's well done. It is a blissful satisfaction in oneself. Though the pleasure given by healthy narcissism is short-lived, it can be rather satisfactory. This reminds me of a song from the West Side Story- "I feel pretty. Oh, so pretty. I feel pretty, witty and bright."

A total obsession with oneself is typical and expected in youngsters at a specific age. The narcissistic period of growth or development starts at around age 2—as children start to cultivate their ability to talk. At this time, children start to utilize words like "I," "mine, " "me" and "no." They tend to behave like the world revolves around them and don't really think much about the needs and wants of anyone except their own.

A famous child psychologist named Margaret Mahler once described this phase as a "love affair with the world." Think of a -year-old running down the road with an expansive grin all over and a rather frantic parent running behind him. If the child's growth goes on as expected, the child will learn through observing his parents, teachers, friends and those around them about the desires, wants and feelings of others. The child's egocentric behavior will diminish while he starts to learn about empathy and understanding.

Healthy narcissism or a "romance with the world" stage is something that grown-ups can hold onto, even if they are no longer the focal point of the universe. It is that cheerful and joyous feeling of enjoying oneself that healthy narcissism is made of.

So, why is healthy narcissism considered to be important?

Healthy narcissism is essential for a variety of reasons. If you can obtain delighted satisfaction in yourself, it will help you through troublesome occasions. For instance, if an individual can get narcissistic joy from a rather tricky task that was well done, it can support that individual through occasions of disappointment while helping them prevent any potential burnout. Similarly, learning to revel in your excellence as well as the positive effect you have on others, can be a great boost to your ego especially when the circumstances are unfavorable.

A lot of people don't develop healthy self-esteem or self-love, and this can happen due to various reasons. Growing up with a self-absorbed parent might mean that most of an individual's childhood was spent catering to the needs of the parent and this left little or no space for the child to learn to celebrate himself. When "Carina" was a kid, she trusted that her mom knew everything and was flawless. As Carina grew up, she discovered that to get some love and praise from her mother, she had to reinforce her mom's faith in her own perfection and flawlessness. In the event that Carina affirmed her own needs, she got brushed off by her mother and her needs were ignored. All this prevented Carina from developing a healthy narcissism.

A few children don't cultivate healthy narcissism since they dread that others will envy them. At the point when a child discovers that they will be rebuffed or treated in an unsightly manner if they perform excellently or surpass any expectations, then he will start to stow away or lessen his excellence and might even start hiding it from himself.

Does it feel wrong to highlight your achievements or take delight in your positive characteristics? Think about all the concerning thoughts that come to your mind like the fear of envy or the worry that others might perceive you as being arrogant. If this is what you experience, then you must reframe these thoughts and start developing healthy narcissism. Learning to be grateful for your talents and being happy in the things you accomplish is desirable and a trait of a healthy mind. In fact, this is quintessential for developing your self-esteem and self-confidence. Remember that there is nothing wrong in appreciating your reflection in the mirror; there is certainly nothing wrong with loving yourself and praising yourself for a job well done.

Severe Narcissism

You might have noticed that the narcissist label is being used quite frequently these days and has become a part of common parlance. It is used in regular conversations, on television and even in articles. Usually, people tend to use it in a negative sense to describe those individuals who seem to think highly of themselves and don't have any regard for the feelings and emotions of others. It is usually used as a put-down and in the realm of politics; it certainly is an assault weapon.

Taking note of the way the term narcissism is normally used, you may get the idea that there is nothing good about narcissism. If this is how you have been viewing narcissism until now, then it is time to change this belief. I am sure that after reading about healthy narcissism, this opinion of yours might have changed a little. Narcissism occurs along a variety of expressions- with healthy narcissism on one end and narcissistic personality disorder on the other end of the spectrum.

From the least to the most poisonous, here are a couple of

different types of extreme narcissism that you might encounter in your life along with some simple ways in which you can deal with such narcissists to prevent any potential conflict.

The understand-It-All Narcissist

This person is always eager to provide his opinion, even when unsolicited, and believes he knows more or is more knowledgeable than everyone else, regardless of the subject in question. He loves to lecture others (usually by offering unsolicited advice) and has a hard time listening because he's too busy considering what he needs to say regarding the subject that's being discussed.

A way to cope: If feasible, forget about his "beneficial" tips or offer a polite thanks and move on. This type of narcissist often tries to show that he is smarter and more informed than anyone else. In fact, a simple way to get out of this is by showing some humility (even if you have to fake it) and show that your point of view is quite flexible and that you are willing to consider all the "insightful" inputs offered by the narcissist. Try to be open to his perspectives but you don't have to endorse them. If you hold onto your sense of humor, then you might notice that the superior or even the condescending manner in which this type of narcissist talks is absurd and even pompous at times.

The Grandiose Narcissist

This is perhaps the most common sort of narcissism that you might encounter. In fact, I am sure that you might have crossed paths with such a narcissist- he sees himself as vital and more influential than anyone else around. He boasts about his own achievements, overemphasizes their significance, and wants to elicit the envy of those around him or is seeking their admiration. He believes he is destined for greatness and brilliant things. When he turns of his charm and charisma, his achievements might be genuinely noteworthy, and you might even discover that you are quite taken with his accomplishments. The only aspect of dealing with such a narcissist which is slightly unpleasant, and irritating is that you are subjected to listening to a never-ending monologue about their so-called superior traits.

A way to cope: His proclamations of superiority may make you want to take a stand for yourself and compete with him. Even if every fiber in your being wants you to do this, please don't. The worst thing that you can do is engage such a narcissist. Even the simplest of efforts from your side to make it seem like you are better than him will encourage him to up his game. Also, by maintaining an air of mystery about yourself, you might be able to discourage the advances of this type of narcissist. He might strike you as a type of celebrity, someone you'd want to work with and serve. Be cautious and don't give away too much information about yourself. One trait that all narcissists share is that they are all self-serving. If they think that they don't stand to gain anything from you, then they wouldn't bat an eye before discarding you.

The Seductive Narcissist

Unlike the previous types of severe narcissist discussed until now, this one manipulates you by enabling you to experience true appreciation for yourself. Initially, he will make it seem like he respects or even idealizes you, but his final purpose is to try and make you feel the same way about him so that he can use you. He might wish to assist, admire and support you to get what he wants. However, when he realizes that he no longer has any use of you, he will discard you rather easily.

A way to cope: It is a good idea to portray yourself as being humble. Don't get carried away by all the flattery, praise or excessive admiration that he showers you with. As wonderful as it may feel to be on the receiving end of such adoration, it does come with certain terms and conditions. In fact, these terms and conditions aren't always disclosed and will land you in a lot of trouble. Notice how he treats all those whom he considers being his rivals or cast-offs. Seeing them experience the callous indifference he treats them with might give you some perspective about what the future of your relationship with him might seem like. As I have already mentioned, once you serve your purpose, you are no longer useful to the narcissist.

The Bullying Narcissist

This kind of a narcissist is someone who makes himself feel better by humiliating others. Even though he might not share the unusual traits that are exhibited by the other types of narcissists discussed until now, he is certainly more brutal in the manner that he declares his superiority in. He will usually rely on contempt to make others feel like they aren't good for anything to make himself feel like a winner. He's going to belittle and ridicule you. Whilst he desires something from you, he may also become threatening if his desires aren't fulfilled. At his absolute worst, this type of narcissist can make you question yourself in all aspects of life and even facilitate the loss of your self-confidence.

A way to cope: As weak as this may sound, the best thing

that you can do is to avoid perturbing his huge ego. Don't fight and don't try to do anything to make him realize that you aren't all that he claims you to be. If he sees you putting up a fight, he might just up the ante and increase the bullying. You can try to stand up for yourself, but don't make it seem too obvious. Well, if none of this seems ideal for you, then the best thing that you can do is try to distance yourself from the said narcissist. In fact, try to put as much distance between the two of you as you possibly can.

The Vindictive Narcissist

With a bullying narcissist, you have the option of coexisting provided you don't seem like an apparent threat to the narcissist. However, with a vindictive narcissist, once you become his target, he will try to do everything that he can to destroy you. You might have probably challenged the said narcissist in some manner that you probably aren't even aware of and all this has made you his target. A vindictive narcissist will try to harm you to merely prove that he is better than you. He might talk trash about you to buddies and own family. He would possibly try and get you fired. If he is your ex-spouse, he may attempt to paint a rather nasty picture of you in front of others.

A way to cope: Whenever feasible, I suggest that you put as much distance between the two of you as you possibly can before he starts hurting your psyche and reputation. Vindictive narcissists try to cover their true nature form everyone expects their victims. So, your survival will usually depend on all the proof that you can muster up against the narcissist. If necessary and if you feel like you are in real trouble, there is no harm in seeking legal help!

Chapter 2: Narcissism in Different Situations

Narcissistic Parents

Do you feel that your parent or caregiver is a narcissist? A lot of parents can be rather difficult to deal with and might even come across as being too overbearing. However, some of them cross this line and tend to enter the territory of being a pathological narcissist. This can effectively turn your entire relationship into a total nightmare. If your parent or caregiver fits this description or exhibits any of the traits that were discussed in the previous chapter, then here are a couple of simple ways in which you can deal with them.

Recognize

Understand and accept the fact that their behavior is impossible to deal with and is no longer merely just "difficult." Most of the people ultimately like to come up with a mutually agreeable solution that can work for all the interested parties. However, someone with narcissistic traits tends to get off on this power play. As long as they feel like they are the ones in control, things will be fine. A lot of people with NPD tend to have a "my way or the highway" kind of attitude. For instance, if a parent refuses to visit his children merely because they didn't opt for the specific career the parent wanted them to pursue is not quite nice. If you feel like your parent is trying to establish unnecessary control over you and the relationship you share with them, then understand that there is nothing normal about it. Also, don't let anyone else tell you otherwise.

Set firm boundaries

A narcissist parent will regularly overstep reasonable boundaries simply to prove that they are able to do so. They may invite themselves to events, make it a point of giving gifts only to those family members they like or even disregard your wishes while interacting with your children. You'll often find that the responsibility of enforcing the consequences for their undesirable behavior rests on your shoulders. It means that you might have to at times say things like "Well, we are happy if you visit us on Thanksgiving, not before that. We don't really want a repeat of what happened last year." You could find yourself feeling as if you're disciplining a toddler, however, this is something that you must do if you want to manage the behavior exhibited by a narcissistic parent.

Prevent yourself from being gas lighted

It's not unusual for a person with NPD to figure out and then try to persuade you that you're loopy or delusional. A friend's mother continuously tells him that he remembers things incorrectly- even though the social worker's documentation supports the friend's claims. A person with NPD might make you believe his version of "reality" and might even convince you that anything that doesn't fit their version isn't true. They might even push you to the extent where you feel like you are losing your mind. Well, you aren't losing your mind and the best thing that you can do is sever ties and distance yourself from such a narcissist.

Others might not understand

Your pals and acquaintances that have no experience of dealing with NPD might dole out advice that is seldom helpful. They might say things like, "after all she is your mother, so you must try to do everything that you can to make things work with her," or "he will eventually come around and understand you." The one thing that you must not permit yourself to do is experience a sense guilty for distancing yourself from a narcissistic parent or worry that others might judge you. Others might offer plenty of advice about how you must deal with your parents, but they aren't the ones living with a narcissistic parent and you are! You are the one that is living with the narcissist and others cannot even begin to comprehend what you are putting up with.

If you feel like things aren't improving and that their narcissistic behavior is taking a toll on you, it is important that you remember to cut ties and walk away. Yes, as cold as it sounds, for your mental and physical well-being, it is quintessential that you sever your ties and walk away.

If you are handling a narcissistic parent, be conscious that you're no longer alone and that there are others who experience similar situations. You can always find help online and connect with others who have experienced all that you are.

Narcissistic Partner

I am living with a narcissist and I would prefer not to leave. "What do I have to know to make this relationship work?"- This happens to be the most common question that a lot of people who are in a relationship with a narcissist tend to have. Well, the most common answer to this question is "simply leave." They have officially decided that their relationship is worth salvaging. They are probably enamored with their narcissistic partner, might have children together or maybe their religious convictions may force them to remain with a partner and do everything conceivable to make the relationship a triumph. Here are the basics things that you must think about if your partner has NPD.

In the event that you are involved with a narcissist, things will be more manageable if you are aware of these three things.

1. What living with a narcissist truly implies?

2. What is practically possible and what isn't,

3. What your limits are.

Living with the narcissist

Enhancement of self-esteem

The principal objective in the life of the vast majority of people who have NPD is the improvement of their self-esteem. Narcissism can be understood as a disorder of self-esteem regulation wherein narcissists are interminably insecure about their status. They may seem certain to you; however, this is just a façade and underneath this façade lies their insecurity about their self-esteem.

Essentially, this implies confidence enhancement, which is eventually more critical to them than you can ever be. At the point when their confidence plunges, narcissists seem to think that they have two options- to either go into a self-detesting melancholy that's based on shame or elevate themselves at the expense of others

Normally, they pick the latter instead of the former. As the individual who is closest to them, they are probably going to belittle you to feel like they are good or superior. A savvy lady once told me, "When they feel fat, they tend to make you feel bad about your weight."

Narcissists need sympathy

An absence of any emotional sympathy or empathy implies that narcissists don't feel terrible when they hurt you. They may not even observe your response. On the off chance that they do, it is quite likely that they will not care. If you do complain or whine about the same, they will shrug off any responsibility and be prepared to listen to something along the lines of, "You are extremely sensitive or touchy." Or they might even accuse you by saying something like, "If you weren't so dumb, I wouldn't need to correct you so frequently."

This implies that they will hurt you- over and again and will do this deliberately as well as unintentionally. You must prepare yourself to deal with all this if you are interested in continuing your relationship with a narcissistic partner.

Incapable of seeing their true selves

Narcissists come up short in their ability to see themselves and other individuals sensibly. Narcissists lack "entire objects relations." "Entire objects relations" is the ability to see both the great and awful characteristics of an individual and acknowledge that both exist. An individual usually develops this characteristic in early childhood by observing and replicating the behavior of their parents and those around them. This is acquired when the individual is seen and loved for whom by his parents and peers regardless of all his imperfections. This ability can be obtained later if the individual with NPD is adequately propelled and has the necessary psychotherapy.

Without "entire objects relations," narcissists shift back and forth between two extraordinary perspectives about themselves and others, which possibly are:

Special, immaculate, supreme, and entitled (all-great), or

Unworthy, imperfect and deficient (all-terrible).

What this implies for you, their partner is that they can't see you in a reasonable and realistic way. To the narcissistic partner, you are either "extraordinary" or "useless." Narcissists can rapidly switch forward and backward between these two elective perspectives about you according to how they feel at the time.

All this has pretty much nothing to do with you. From the get-go in the relationship, the narcissistic partner is probably going to consider you to be immaculate, faultless and exceptional (all great). At that point, as he becomes more acquainted with you and starts to see your flaws that all humans have and the ways in which you differ from his idea of the perfect mate, he will probably change his previous opinion about you and might start to think of you as being imperfect and flawed. This makes any happiness that you two ever feel together brief and delicate. Your happiness or the one that you and your partner experience together is based on the narcissist and since he is extremely touchy and unfit to keep up a steady and positive picture of you, he will end up feeling dissatisfied and upset.

Narcissists don't have any "object consistency." It essentially implies that the minute that your narcissistic partner feels something negative, it disturbs the positive association he might have of you and everything that's positive flies out the window. Your entire positive history with them and all the good that you have ever done for them will become inconsequential. You will be left thinking about how this can possibly happen: one moment your partner is thoroughly adoring and you two are quite happy and then the next minute it seems like he hates you or is upset with you.

The appropriate response is that the absence of "object consistency" is an outcome of not having "whole objects relations."

Keep in mind that they cannot view you as someone who is a whole person with qualities that are both good and bad. The only thing that a narcissistic partner can do is constantly switch between adoring and hating you. This shift is fully dependent on that aspect of your persona or behavior comes to the forefront at the time. Think about it like a camera that can just observe what is going on in the present. The past does not exist for a camera. For instance, let us look at a hypothetical scenario to get a better understanding of what it feels like to live with a narcissistic partner.

Rosie and Al were perched on the couch viewing their favorite sitcom together. They were quite happy and were nestled together on the couch. Rosie got up to go to the kitchen for something and Al felt irritated about her leaving. He thought: "How could she interrupt while we were watching TV together? She can't seem to think about how I feel if she just leaves the room!" Al started to get increasingly more irritated as he thought more about it. When Rosie returned, he was enraged and needed to rebuff her. All the pleasant feelings he had about her just a couple of minutes ago disappeared.

Rosie (who was still feeling warm and fuzzy about Al) returned and sat down alongside him hoping to pick up where they had earlier let off. Instead of getting her up to speed about the details of the sitcom, an irritate Al stated, "How could you leave that way! You are so rude. Don't you care at all about how I feel?" Needless to state, the remainder of the night did not go well and by the time they went to bed, they were no longer talking to each other.

In the event that you might be involved with a narcissist, you have to prepare yourself for circumstances like the one that I mentioned above. They are unavoidable. Since you and your narcissistic partner are two distinct individuals with completely different thinking processes and sensitivities, it is quite likely that some remark or behavior can trigger your narcissistic partner's insecurity. When this does happen, all the nice feelings will vanish, and your partner will start to despise you and might even start degrading you. A couple of minutes ago, everything was fine, but now you might find yourself in a hostile situation. This leads me to the second point of dealing with a narcissistic partner.

What Is Possible and What Isn't

Narcissists can never acknowledge their fault

Since narcissists see just two options, they are either immaculate or useless. In fact, it is quite unlikely that the narcissistic partner might accept any of their mistakes. They seem to think that accepting their faults or mistakes renders them useless. If they do this, then their self-esteem will take a plunge off the deep end and they will start hating themselves. They might also think that by accepting their fault, it will make you hate them, and this worsens the way they feel about themselves. Let us continue with the hypothetical scenario we were discussing in the previous point.

The following morning Al wakes up in a good mood and goes to give Rosie a warm hug. He is rather stunned when she dismisses his physical advances. "What's the issue with her?" he pondered. Obviously, the previous evening's quarrel was out of his mind because his spirits are now high, and he is feeling good. However, now Rosie is blaming him for starting a ridiculous fight that fully ruined what could have been a perfect night for them.

Rosie needed Al to assume his responsibility for starting the fight. Al, being a narcissist automatically assumed this as Rosie needing him to feel embarrassed and instead of accepting his fault, he abruptly shifts the entire blame onto her. He says, "If you hadn't abruptly decided to leave, things would have been perfectly fine. It was because of you that we fought." Now, this just rekindles the fight once again.

Narcissists don't apologize

Since narcissists think that it is too mortifying to even think about accepting their fault, they will probably never be eager to apologize- regardless of being aware that they were the ones who were at fault. So, if you have any illusions about your narcissistic partner apologizing to you, I suggest that you get rid of such thoughts. It is implausible to even expect an apology from a narcissist.

Narcissists will usually make some sort of a sweet gesture later on and that is their equivalent of an apology. So, your partner's idea of apologizing to you might be buying you a gift or taking you out for a meal. That's about it and you must not express any grand gesture of apology. If you are interested in prolonging the relationship, then I suggest that you learn to acknowledge their reparative signal without requesting a verbal expression of their remorse. Let us continue with the hypothetical scenario we were discussing in the previous point.

So, Al goes ahead and realizes that maybe he added to their fight and might have overreacted. To compensate for his outburst, he decides to gift Rosie a pretty bracelet that he knows she will appreciate. That night, he gives her the box with the bracelet and tells her that it reminded him of her. Rosie fusses over the gift and is quite taken. She happily takes it from him and even kisses him to show her happiness. In this situation, she realizes that this was Al's way of apologizing and accepts it.

Pick your fights

You must prepare yourself to let any minor and unintended rudeness goes. It is ideal if you carefully pick your fights. If you tell your narcissistic partner each and every time he offends or hurts you, the relationship will quickly turn sour and you will find yourself caught up in a constant spew of fights and you stand to gain nothing from all this. To save yourself from the misery of all those fights and deliberate put-downs, you must wisely choose your fights. You can save all those fights for any serious issues or deliberate insults that prompt you to end the relationship. What's more, you must prepare yourself to sever ties with your narcissistic partner if he fails to refuse those limits. Most of the narcissists will continue to do and act as they please if you allow them to.

Narcissists are reluctant to process past fights

After a fight with your partner, you might need to return and talk about what went wrong and how you can prevent it the next time around. Your narcissistic partner might not be willing to comply with this since it tends to make him feel like you are shaming him by rubbing his nose in it. Here are a couple of different things that you can do to prevent this from happening.

Start using "we" language since it works better. If you start using "we" while discussing a fight or the things that went wrong, it will not make your partner feel like you are singling him out and will instead reassure him that you were both to be blamed. For instance, you can try saying something like, "I know we both adore one another and need things to go well. I believe that we can both concur that in the future we must make an effort to be kind to each other and a little careful about the way in which we express ourselves."

Set Your Boundaries and Protect Them

Narcissists have no regard for others limits

This implies that you must be clear about what kind of narcissistic behavior is tolerable for you and what isn't. When left to their own devices, narcissists will try to cross the boundaries of other individuals. For instance, a narcissistic partner might not think twice before criticizing about the way you dress, your family members or even about anything else that is dear to you. In fact, a narcissist might say things that will hit you below the belt and say mean things to you. After all, that's said and done, he might start behaving like nothing of that sort had ever happened. Here is a hypothetical situation that will help you get a better understanding.

Betty's beau David discovered proof that while he was away on a trek, she reconnected with a former sweetheart of hers. When he went up and confronted her about the same, she retorted by saying, "you are quite revolting and ugly. In fact, I am doing you a favor by engaging in sexual acts with you. You must be grateful that you have me and must stop complaining." Ouch! That does sound rather harsh and mean, doesn't it?

Betty was astounded when David said that she had crossed a limit and that he didn't want to see her again. When she understood that he meant it for real, she begged him to stay with her and to give her another chance to prove herself to him.

Betty was truly fond of David and was just reflexively repeating the kind of behavior she had seen her mother dish out toward her father while growing up. It never crossed her mind that she was crossing a limit and that David might just take her words seriously and leave her. In her mind, the words that she uttered amounted to nothing and she was simply rebuffing David for standing up to her with the proof of her infidelity.

Some narcissists have no qualms about creating a mortifying scene publicly

This can vary from them irately demanding that you two get up and leave an eatery since they feel like the service is personally insulting, even though you are quite happy with staying to them shouting at you on a crowded street and walking away.

You have to choose if this is something you can live with at all and, assuming this is, where the limit is for you. Any narcissist who does this once is probably going to do this again. It is a way for them to cope with something that they perceive to be insulting to their self-worth.

Here is another scenario for you to consider.

Patty is quite pretty, and she is aware of it. She is quite narcissistic and feels like she is entitled to do and say as she pleased when she pleased. She realized that most men were usually grateful to share her company.

Chad is out on a first date with Patty. She gets offended because of something he says and leaves him sitting in the restaurant all by himself. She expects Chad to race up to her, apologize for saying what he did and beg her to return to their date. Instead, Chad decides to stay back and orders for a drink. In a while, he messages Patty saying, "I didn't have any intention of offending you. We should probably start over. Why don't you come back? Let us enjoy a meal together and see where this goes?"

Patty acknowledged his conciliatory sentiment and returns to the table (and they continue to have a rather lovely night. They both keep up the pretense that nothing happened and carry on. Chad earned Patty's respect by not pursuing her and furthermore by the quiet and sharp way in which he dealt with her terrible conduct. For Chad, the limit was clear. He did as much as he was happy to do. If Patty had decided to not return, then he would not have been interested in going on a second date with her.

Verbal misuse may raise to physical maltreatment

In the event that you don't draw any limits around verbal maltreatment, your partner may progress to manhandle you physically. Except if you are a masochist and appreciate being beaten, I propose you stop them from doing anything like this from the beginning itself. It might begin fairly harmlessly, but it will rapidly progress if you don't draw a line and allow them to continue. Let us look at a hypothetical situation for better understanding.

Netta and Harry were hitched for a year when he advanced from shouting at her when he was irritated to snatching her arm. Netta reassured herself by saying that he was simply weary and had no intention of hurting her, so she let this go.

It wasn't an isolated incident and it happened once again when they were out to supper with another couple. Harry didn't like something that Netta said and kicked her hard under the table. She noisily stated, "Ouch, stop that!" Embarrassed, Harry frowned at her for the remainder of the night and barely talked. It turned out to be a rather strained meal with Netta. The other couple tried quite hard to pretend as though nothing happened and things were absolutely fine.

When Harry and Netta returned home, he began shouting at her. According to him, he was the victim. He said to Netta, "Don't you ever do that to me again in public or I will hurt you." This was when Netta realized that he had crossed a genuine limit and she figured out that the best thing to do was that she takes a stand for herself if she didn't want their marriage to turn into a horrific experience.

She told Harry, "Harry, I cherish you and I need to make

our marriage work. You have to realize that it isn't acceptable to me if you lay a hand on me, ever again. I don't care about how distraught you were feeling. I am more than open to discuss all this, and I will apologize if I am not right."

Harry attempted to rationalize and shift the blame onto her for everything. Netta persevered until she got him to agree that he could never lay a hand on her again or undermine her with the threat of physical violence. Harry acknowledged Netta was not kidding and that if he wanted her to not divorce him, then he must be cautious about the way he treated her."

There is nothing that's simple about being in a relationship with a narcissist. It will nonetheless be a smoother experience if you can accept what to expect from your partner, arm yourself with a couple of tips about dealing with a narcissist and set some boundaries for yourself.

Narcissistic Boss

For all intents and purposes, everybody has either worked for a narcissistic boss or been involved with one in some form or the other. I am certain that it is a rather unforgettable experience to work for someone who is blatantly self-centered, conceited and self-absorbed. To work for someone who works only when someone is noticing, who is quick to accept all the credit and quickly shift the blame onto others.

A narcissistic boss will spend a great deal of his time thinking about attaining power, influence as well as success. As a result of all this, there will always be a propensity to not just lie, but even over-exaggerate one's self-importance.

Yet, the most concerning issue with having a narcissistic boss is that they never feel they're the issue. They might have a couple of convenient employees whom they use as scapegoats or might even try to pick someone randomly to blame them when things go south.

In case you're working for a narcissistic boss, you fundamentally have two options: you either quit and land another position or you stay put and learn to deal with it. If you decide to stay put, then the only way to deal with your boss is to change the way you react or respond to him since there is possibly no way in which you can change him. In this section, you will learn about different tips that you can follow to ensure that you are able to deal with your narcissistic boss without going crazy.

Comprehend the source

To adapt to your narcissistic boss, you must try to understand him. The chances are quite high that they're never going to change, and they're never going to be anything but difficult to work with. Be prepared to deal with things that sound like the following.

That didn't occur.

Well, even if it did, I am sure it wasn't that terrible.

Furthermore, if it did, it wasn't that big a deal.

And if it was, then I am not the one to be blamed.

And if that did too, then I didn't mean it.

And, if it did, then you are to be blamed and not me.

React, don't respond

While dealing with a narcissist the worst thing that you can possibly do is shift attention onto their terrible behavior. Keep in mind that narcissists thrive when they are given attention. Instead of doing things that will give them attention, the bests thing that you can do is learn to respond in a way that ensures that the power to decide and choose still lies with you. Try not to react. If you react, you are merely giving the control away to the narcissist. Instead, you must learn to respond after you consider the consequences of your potential reaction.

Set clear limits

Set a firm limit wherever you need one and stick to it. Keep in mind, limits aren't intended to control others; they're a rule for you to realize what is and isn't acceptable to you. Limits are a means of taking care of yourself and they are normal as well as necessary.

Don't let them bother you

Try not to let them get under your skin. Narcissists love getting a rise out of someone- especially someone they hold power over. The narcissist might try to goad you, call you out or even try to humiliate you, but you always have control and have the ability to not allow any of these things bother you. This is when you must use your emotional intelligence to ensure that you are controlling your thoughts and actions. In fact, nothing bothers a narcissist more than being unable to get a reaction from someone.

Don't encourage

A narcissistic boss has a rather constant need of being respected and admired by others. So, you must do everything that you can to not encourage this need of his. It will be quite wise to understand that bad behavior usually stems from insecurities. The more the narcissist acts out, the more insecure they truly are. However, it is quintessential to remember that the more you encourage their unfavorable behavior, the worse will it become. Narcissists usually like to surround themselves with just two sorts of individuals: the individuals who empower them and the individuals who keep quiet. Any individual who doesn't fit into one of these two classifications will surely be fired or even banished. If the narcissist manages to get his way, it is likely that he will make you believe that everything was your fault.

Don't engage

Try not to engage the individuals who don't deserve it. Your narcissistic boss holds some level of authority over you by the virtue of his position. It will do you good to remember that a leader cannot exist without followers. So, make it a point to not follow those you don't admire, trust and respect. Simply do your job to the best of your abilities and do with all the respect, deference and integrity that you can muster. When you do this, you will be known as one of the sane ones at work- may be the only rational one.

Check everything

A narcissist will certainly depict himself as a victim who is innocent and honest in all matters. If the truth offends him, this does happen more frequently than he would care for, he will quickly change it to suit his needs. while dealing with a narcissistic boss, you must make it a point to check up on all facts before blinding trusting what he says.

Try not to argue

The things that a narcissist might say will want you to react in some form or the other. The last thing that you must do is get into a battle of words with a narcissist. If you do this, then keep in mind that everything that you say and do will is obviously used against you. Don't argue or engage with your narcissistic boss, instead try to make them invisible and prevent yourself from becoming an obvious target. It's difficult to argue with somebody who will misshape reality to suit their needs.

Try not to be provoked

Provoking someone and then blaming them for a fight is something that narcissists enjoy. Remain cool, unaffected and refuse to get carried away by the provocation that the narcissist tries to throw your way. Try not to allow yourself to be provoked or controlled.

Focus

Stay concentrated on what's important. Working with a narcissist boss means that he will try to do everything that he can to make sure that you play by his rules and that he is the center of attention, at all times. It is quite easy to get caught up with all this and even get upset when the narcissist conveniently shifts the blame onto others for his shortcomings. So, instead of becoming his pawn by reacting, the best thing that you can do is concentrate only on those things that are important to you.

It's never going to be simple while you are dealing with a narcissist. The wisest thing that you can do is walk away, if that's not an option, then remember to follow the simple tips given in this section to effectively deal with a narcissistic boss.

Narcissism at Workplace

Narcissism is definitely not a psychological issue or an ailment. It is present in each individual, but in varying degrees. You can be the delighted worker, surrounded by happy colleagues and all that's good, but the guys you need to watch out for will not wear a funny suit surrounded by minions singing his praises.

Among your charming network of friends, there might be individuals who will compliment you, bolster you and even chuckle alongside you, while they are utilizing this opportunity to covertly dig a hole for you to accidentally stumble into.

What makes these folks very dangerous is their innate ability to control a circumstance in such a manner that you end up looking terrible, while they shine- shine brightly like the freshly sharpened dagger's blade that's waiting to just stab someone. On the off chance that you spend quite some time with them, then you might start feeling absolutely worthless. These individuals are skilled at controlling their feelings and only showcasing what they want the world to see. A narcissist will never reveal his true intentions. They will string you along such that before you realize it, they will have already trapped you.

Things being what they are, who are these psychological manipulators I am talking about? Is it a defining trait of narcissists or sociopaths? Are we all the unsuspecting victims of such individuals or is there a possible way to discern them before they do any damage? Therefore, you must try to recognize the usual methods that are employed by a narcissist to obtain what he desires.

Here is a rundown of the different kinds of manipulative tactics that a manipulator might resort to while at work.

Fortify your certainty

The narcissist must obtain the attention of everybody around him. So, if you come across someone and you feel like the said person is going out of his way to charm your socks off, then please tread carefully. Narcissists tend to start off by giving you all the possible compliments to get you hooked onto them. When this is done, they can string you along and play you like a violin.

Despite the fact that you may find it very exciting and your ego might be stoked, it is better to keep your feet planted firmly on the ground instead of getting carried away by the things the narcissist says. Two or three enticing words can be the ideal snare that a narcissist can use to make you accept their workload and work on that huge assignment that they have procrastinating since a while. a lot of work and work on that monstrous task that they have been putting on hold. If you go down this path, then remember that it will a long and arduous journey with little or nothing to gain.

Shaking your world

How often did you notice something negative that a friend, colleague or a relative of yours did or said with the sole purpose of embarrassing or ridiculing you? The classic narcissist will try to change your reality and make it seem like all the embarrassment and the ridicule that you experienced was only a figment of your imagination and wasn't real? Also, experiencing events like this will make you feel like you are slowly losing your mind. If they keep at it long enough, you will come to doubt everything and might start to think that you are living in an alternate universe where the narcissist is the scriptwriter.

Projection of flaws

A narcissist uses something that's known as "projection" to gain control over his unsuspecting victim. A narcissistic will try to ensure that all his flaws are nothing but a mere projection of your flaws on him. This is a tactic that a manipulator will resort to for explaining his wrongdoings and he does this by conveniently shifting the blame onto his unsuspecting victim's shoulders.

It is quite similar to the tactics that a cheating spouse might use- "I am not the one that's cheating, and it is merely in your head. You are being clingy and by suspecting my fidelity you are ruining a perfectly good relationship. It is all in your head and so on and so forth." It is like the head of a government stating that he could have governed his country better if it wasn't for the reluctance of people and their incessant questioning about everything that he tries to do. Instead of shouldering the blame for their incompetence, they will try to make others feel like they are the ones who are wrong. For instance, a narcissistic employee might say something like "If you had assigned a better project to me, I might have done a better job. Clearly, you aren't a good enough manager."

Diversion to win arguments

A common technique of manipulation that narcissists use is to direct an argument or a conversation in a different direction and divert it from the initial issue by asking or bringing up issues that are sensitive. A narcissist uses this technique to divert other's minds from picking up on their flaws. The primary idea of the narcissist is to confuse or even frustrate you by using some type of a grandstanding opinion that is quite different from the former topic in question. This type of behavior sprouts from a rather insecure place in their psyche. The thought of a disagreement is a perceived threat to a narcissist's idea of self-professed grandeur. Usually, politicians tend to use this technique to instigate the masses against their opposition- "If you don't agree with the existing policies, then you are a true patriot." Well, you get the idea, don't you?

Deprecating your opinion

In a rather lousy attempt of trying to criticize your opinion, a narcissist might call you something bad so that he doesn't have to think too hard or put up a fight. With the increasing popularity of social media these days, you might have noticed the onslaught of cyber bullies who tend to deprecate the opinions of their targets. Most of the statements that they make aren't backed by any rational argument and don't present an alternate opinion. They are simply made with the idea of belittling their target. The idea of the narcissist is to keep away from logic and keep everything foggy, so no one puts up a fight.

Extreme labeling

Narcissists tend to make declarations that are often absurd

and at times outrageous to merely point out your bias. What is their motive? Well, they resort to this to show how unfair you are. For instance, let us assume that your colleague is making crude remarks about your sense of dressing. You might simply point out that he is being crude. If the said colleague is a narcissist, then it is quite likely that he will come up with an extreme label to show your unfairness (even if it doesn't exist). So, such a person might say something like "Are you really this sensitive?"

Never appreciate

Nothing you ever do will ever be agreeable for a narcissist. In the event that it is acceptable, at that point you stop being his punching bag. Without you to feed his inflated ego, he will need to go through the entire process of finding another human punching bag to replace you. Here are a couple of ways in which a conversation with a narcissist using this technique might go like.

Is it difficult to be single at this age?

Oh no, when did you get hitched?

You've been married for such a long time but don't have any kids?

Oh Goodness, you do? Oh, so they are a teenager? How wonderful…

Does it bother you that they will soon be young adults who will need to get married soon?

Phew, there is certainly no way in which you can please a narcissist.

Rude jokes and offensive sarcasm

Narcissistic individuals like to belittle their targets by making jokes or using sarcasm that is considered to be offensive. They will usually do this in the presence of others or when they have an audience. What's the purpose of all this? Well, the premise is to make themselves look clever while making a fool of you. Narcissists like taking shots at others without any remorse.

Cheapen your achievements

Narcissists can act quite slowly and play a long con. They might take all the time that's needed to gain your trust, make you trust them and believe that they truly value you. Once they achieve this, they will start to alienate you from everything that you enjoy so that they are the ones with absolute control over you. They might even use the falsified claims of apparent third parties to make you feel like you aren't good enough.

Narcissists can play mind games unlike anyone else. Their toxic games are beyond the comprehension of a normal mind. The narcissist will not only try to provoke his target by taking some unjust digs at them but will also make the victim like their reaction (even when justified) was absolutely uncalled for. Not just that, a narcissist will constantly try to push you to your limit. He usually does this to see how much you can tolerate and how far he can push you. If he realizes that he can break past your boundaries without any reprimand, he will keep at it.

Chapter 3: Dealing with Narcissists

Manipulative Tactics Narcissists Use

In this section, you will learn about the common tactics that a narcissist uses against their victims.

The world of a narcissist is quite complex. The disorder that they suffer from is unlike any other and it can confuse all those around them and prevent them from understanding what is happening. How is it that narcissists are quite good at manipulating others?

Narcissists are good at manipulating others because they are always trying to look for the vulnerabilities that others have. Once they understand what is important to you, they will try to use those things against you. Some instances of vulnerabilities include your family members, any self-esteem issues or even insecurities you might have about your appearance and such, or even the fear of being alone or losing someone close to you. narcissists will try to find out these vulnerabilities that their victims have during the stages of the relationship in which they are going through the love bombing and the good listener phases.

Narcissists try to target those who are codependent; someone who may have experienced a rather abusive relationship or might have grown up in homes with narcissistic members of the family; They may have many other problems with self-esteem and self-control, but to be honest, I think the main reason why people stay in relation to the narcissus is that they simply do not realize they are in a relationship with someone who is a narcissist.

Normal people operate in what sociologists call the "just world." This "fair world" perspective means that we tend to think that the way we treat people is how they will treat us, that the world is "fair" or just, and that our moral and values are similar to those around us. And this point of view is true in the vast majority of cases, except when dealing with manipulation, such as those who have narcissistic or sociopathic/antisocial personalities.

Once again, we act from the perspective of the "just world," where we think that if we do something harmful or malicious, we would change that. However, the truth is that narcissists as well as sociopaths do not care if their behavior can hurt others, in fact, they often get great pleasure in causing pain. In the end, the more reactions they can elicit from others, the greater will they feel, and their ego tends to get a kick out of it as well.

There is no better manipulator than the narcissists especially if they are "hidden." A narcissist/ secret sociopath will pretend (convincingly) that he has the same manners and values as the rest of society, and all with the ultimate goal of making us have access to everything they can wish for: sex, attention, money, food, clothing, housing, status, etc. however, the truth is that they do not have the same morality and values that we do. They have no morals or values at all, although they can pretend. They can even do everything possible to show the world that they have moral values and values higher than the rest of us, take a position of power in their church, volunteer regularly and verbally denounces those who show some kind. Ethically doubtful behavior or the desire that others perceive them as a wonderful person, friend, colleague, father, neighbor. But over time, those who really know a narcissist will begin to realize that they have the duality of Dr. Jekyll / Mr. Hyde in them, that their words are very different from their actions, all the things they so strongly declare They are exactly what they do.

In short, narcissists are no more than emotional delinquents.

It takes some time for normal people to realize this because the likelihood that our partner is an emotional manipulator is not on our radar. Therefore, when a narcissist displays any negative behavior, you might treat him in the same way as another normal person who has displayed undesirable behavior- you will try to work through this; you offer him a second chance; you try to understand if you played in things; you decide that you both must go to therapy, marriage counseling and read self-help books. You understand that relationships take effort and that all relationships tend to have their ups and downs. And maybe, in the depths of your soul, you believe that there is something of value in going through all the nonsense and are happy to be together through all this. Many victims adhere to these beliefs for years, sometimes decades, until they get tired of riding this carousel and decide to split.

You might even experience some guilt for leaving before you start learning about narcissists and sociopaths, and then all of their behavior begins to take on full meaning. Once you become aware of all this, you might feel stupid for staying so long. (Even if you feel that this is normal, do not be so hard on yourself. You did not know you were in a relationship with a person with a personality disorder).

So, how can you distinguish a normal relation from a narcissistic relationship?

What distinguishes narcissistic relationships from normal relationships is that normal people in normal relationships express real regret for their misbehavior, offer to compensate for their misbehavior through consistent actions and live transparently until their partner accepts that they do not live transparently.

In a narcissistic relationship, you will notice that a narcissist will not offer any sincere apologies (if you get any!), will not have a desire to change, that only lasts while you are angry, and continues to sneak away and live their lives as they see fit. In a normal, healthy relationship, the same problems (usually lies, fraud, abuse- verbal or emotional) do not happen again and again.

Here are the six manipulation techniques that a narcissist will often use.

Denial

As soon as you confront a narcissist about their bad behavior, a narcissist will immediately deny it like it never even happened- even if you present solid evidence. If you do manage to get the narcissist to admit anything, they will try to admit only the bare minimum and will deny all the bad bits or admit things only to the extent that they know that you are aware of. victims stay in a relationship with a manipulative person who doesn't own up to his or her actions, then the victims start to question their perceptions and will start to question whether the thing that they are talking about really did happen or not. narcissists, as well as sociopaths, are such good manipulators and are quite popular for the gas lighting techniques they use, that the victim is often partial towards believing their perspectives instead of trusting what they saw or experienced. If denial doesn't do the trick for the narcissist, then they will try to combine it with all the other strategies discussed in this section.

Triangulation

Triangulation is a favorite tool for all manipulators, and it is quite similar to a love triangle, except that it doesn't necessarily involve any lovers. This can happen in any relationship dynamic that involves three individuals- at work, at home or even with friends. A triangle is formed in such a way with two people, that they are pitted against each other by the narcissist so that each thinks the other is responsible for the trouble and it leaves the real culprit out of the equation. A narcissist parent can turn two of his children against each other or a narcissist husband can pit his wife against some other woman. This trick is brilliant in its simplicity and quite evil. This helps to keep the narcissist in the clear and free of all blame and all the frenzy and confusion it creates clearly boosts the narcissist's ego. In fact, the narcissist tends to get a kick out of seeing that they are being fought over or from the knowledge that they have sufficient power to control and upset others.

Pity

Never underestimate a narcissist. They know that if they can get you to feel sorry for them, then they will be able to manipulate you in such a way that it can shift your focus from their negative behavior to instead focus on making them feel better. The narcissist might try to gain your sympathy by playing the card of a bad childhood, excessive stress at work, and a terrible past relationship or even alcoholism. They might even tell the victim that they have suicidal tendencies and depression. They can come up with rather inventive lies to distract their victim from their bad behavior. There are no limits to the lengths that a narcissist can go to achieve this goal. their conscience clearly doesn't get in their way.

Guilt

"It is your fault." This is the go-to line for almost all narcissists. Somehow and in some manner, the cheating, lying or any other form of bad behavior that the narcissist exhibits are all your fault. They can easily make their victim feel the guilt for pointing out something that is obviously wrong. Perhaps your partner is telling you that you need to stay more at home, avoid going out with your friends late at night, avoid drinking or even wear some specific clothes. According to the narcissist, his or her behavior is always the fault of the victim. The narcissist will be quick to point out that whatever they did or said was due to your mistakes and not theirs. An abusive partner, after a rather violent outburst, tends to blame the victim by saying that the victim made him do a specific thing. A narcissist is always careful with the words he or she uses. Even when they are lying, they tend to ensure that whatever they are saying has some truth to it so that they can guilt trip their partners.

Intimidation

They tend to make threats that are thinly veiled, or they can even come right out and threaten you. Intimidation doesn't always have to be physical in nature. It can even be in the form of a threat that the partner might report you for being an unfit parent, threatening to divorce you or anything like that. Of course, there are other forms of intimidation like stalking or even the threat of physical violence does the trick at times. A narcissist will always go to great lengths to ensure that they will get what they want. Victims often stay in a relationship with a narcissist because they are too scared to leave and are worried about what the narcissist will do.

Hope

A narcissist can put on an Oscar-winning performance to get their victims to believe that all that they need is another chance to prove that they have changed. It is quite understandable why the victims tend to believe them and fall for their lies and false promises. Hope is eternal and even if there is a sliver of hope that the narcissist might change, the victims tend to stick around.

This brings me back to the concept of "just world"- a perspective that normal people tend to have. Normal people believe that their actions if hurtful must be mended and they will be sorry for their acts. A narcissist, on the other hand, will simply make his or her victims feel that they are sorry (it is only temporary and will not last). A narcissist's behavior might be so outlandish that it might make the victim feel like they have hit rock bottom. Well, let me tell you something, with a narcissist there is no rock bottom. They are capable of making decisions based solely on their whims and fancies and nothing else.

There is no way in which you can fix a narcissists behavior. All that you can do is ensure that you distance yourself from such a toxic relationship. It is time that you start thinking about yourself and stop placing anyone else above you. You have the power to right by you, so you must.

Narcissistic Injury

The narcissistic injury takes place when narcissists respond adversely to apparent or genuine criticism, any limits set on them, as well as any endeavors made to hold them accountable for their conduct. It also happens when an individual refuse to oblige to a narcissist's unquenchable need for admiration, praise or anything that the narcissist desires. The "damage" also occurs when the narcissist over-intensifies or personalizes normal interactions or when an individual without any malignant intentions doesn't meet the narcissist's desire to attain elevated levels of praise or recognition.

The "injury" is usually trailed by the narcissist's loss of control over his emotional composure and a consequent outburst of passive or vindictive reactions. These episodes of emotional outbursts are referred to as emotional deregulation since these emotional reactions are often out of the narcissist's control.

The term that's used to describe any threat to the oversized ego or inflated self-esteem of a narcissist is known as narcissistic injury. Keep in mind that all those who suffer from NPD tend to have a rather twisted sense of their self-importance and seem to think of themselves as superior beings who are entitled to anything that they desire. They tend to live in a make-believe world where they are the epitome of all things good- success, power, intelligence, tact or even beauty. They seem to believe that they are quite unique and deserve all the attention in the world. They need constant praise, admiration as well as attention. All this, in turn, acts as fodder for their inflated egos. Well, this is a vicious cycle with seemingly no end.

Anything that the narcissist views as a threat to their inflated sense of ego or their s-called dominance, is believed to be a narcissistic injury. The word "perceived" is quintessential because it means that the threat might not be real, for instance, an average individual might not think of it as a threat or a challenge, but a narcissist will certainly think of it as a threat. A real or apparent threat might be something like others pointing out one of the narcissist's lies, challenging his dominance or even saying something along the lines that make the narcissist feel like his needs aren't a priority. Things that a narcissist might think of as an injury include such instances like when someone makes a remark about the narcissist not being the best-dressed individual, by pointing something that the narcissist can do better or whenever someone disagrees with the narcissist's opinion or point of view. Usually, these things are quite common and are a part of daily conversations. However, for a narcissist, all these things are belittling and will not think of them as harmless opinions. An ordinary individual might even brush off these instances as a regular conversation, but this ceases to happen for a narcissist.

At times, the injury can be caused when someone doesn't do or say something. Whenever a narcissist does something, he expects to be praised and appreciated for what he's done, regardless of how inconsequential or trivial the thing is. An average individual might not make a big deal of it and will not be bothered if others don't acknowledge all that he'd done. For a narcissist, the lack of appreciation or compliments is perceived as an insult or even criticism for what he's done, and he will respond as if it was an insult.

Ways to Handle A Narcissist

A propensity toward narcissism is present in all of us and

the degree to which it is present determines whether it is healthy narcissism or extreme narcissism. At times, you might not even have the slightest idea of how great an individual's narcissistic traits are until you have come to establish a deep bond with the said individual or are in a relationship with them. Only then will you realize that all those traits that previously attracted you to that individual are the ones that you aren't able to deal with now. You might have a parent, sibling or some family member whose narcissistic traits you must deal with, but you cannot control. You might be forced to work with a boss, a colleague, a teacher, a student or even an employee who displays extreme traits of narcissism.

Because a few people show narcissistic tendencies doesn't mean they cannot be loved. Individuals with levels of narcissism might be fun, alluring, or great at what they do. Having them around gives you more joy than agony and, in the work environment, it uplifts your group's prosperity. You may, if given a choice in the issue, like the idea of reforming the said narcissist instead of cutting him off from your life altogether.

Not all narcissists are made alike, so the manner in which you handle one in your life ought to be found on which type you're managing. College of Nottingham therapist Vincent Egan and teammates (2014), scrutinized a sample of over 850 online subjects to determine the connection between emotional wellbeing and tendencies of narcissism. Researchers had earlier distinguished between two different forms of narcissists- the vulnerable and the grandiose kinds.

The outward shell of a vulnerable narcissist or the outward projection of self-absorption and elevated sense of self-centeredness are a means of masking a weak inner self. Whereas a grandiose narcissist is an individual who believes that he is great and at times, they might actually be as good as they seem to think they are.

These two things are types of narcissism, however, those with a grandiose kind of narcissism tend to display the traits dubbed as the "dark triad" along with the traits of psychopathy (the lack of guilt or empathy) and Machiavellianism (manipulative behavior). The dark triad is the phrase that's used to describe the need to seek praise and special treatment from others (narcissism), to be insensitive (psychopathy) and manipulative (Machiavellianism). According to Eagan and his team, all those individuals with high levels of narcissism as well as Machiavellianism, are the ones that can truly get under your skin. Their antagonistic attitude towards life makes it quite difficult to live with them and they will almost always intrude while you are trying to attain your goals. Machiavellian narcissists have aced the specialty of one-uppance as they endeavor to demonstrate their superiority while trampling all over other's feelings as well as emotions.

Egan and colleagues called attention to the fact that no past research had taken a look at the role of feelings, particularly positive feelings, in studies or research about the Dark Triad. They were of the opinion that narcissism may have varying connections to happiness than would psychopathy and Machiavellianism. At the end of the day, it may be conceivable to be a happy narcissist—yet less conceivable to be a cheerful sociopath or manipulator.

In their study, the participants were asked to rate themselves by giving them a personality test that asked them to rate themselves based on five factors- traits of extroversion, agreeableness, and openness to experience, conscientiousness and emotional stability. Apart from this, they were also asked to rate themselves for their dark triad traits. The subjective well being of the participants of the study was rated using one scale that measured happiness and the other that measured satisfaction with life.

In the wake of consolidating and analyzing the scores according to these measures, Egan's group managed to distinguish and identify 4 bunches groups in the sample they were studying- vulnerable narcissists, a group that was identified by their unhappiness, grandiose narcissists and one that was identified by their low levels of narcissism and general happiness.

Contrasting the two categories of narcissists, Egan, and his associates found that the grandiose narcissists would, in general, be more joyful, increasingly outgoing, and all the more emotionally steady. The vulnerable narcissists were less pleasant, less emotionally steady, and ranked higher in the other Dark Triad qualities of being manipulative and psychopathy. With these discoveries as the foundation, now we can look at the ways in which you can deal with your own feelings when you're managing individuals high in narcissism.

Understand the type

Figure out which type you're managing. Vulnerable narcissists don't feel especially great about themselves on a fundamental level. when compared to the grandiose narcissists, they are less "out there" with their feelings, thus you probably won't understand when they're undermining you or getting in your way. In case you're trying to make the most of the individuals in your family or in your workgroup to the best probable use, the grandiose narcissist may be your best partner—as long as you can get that individual to agree to the group's overall goals.

Recognize your irritation

As noted above, the antagonistic traits of a narcissist can get under your skin. In case you are attempting to complete something, and one individual is continually hindering or is trying to shift the spotlight onto himself, then you must learn to recognize the cause for your frustration. Once you understand the reason, it lends you the power to put an end to it all.

Acknowledge where the conduct originates from

Vulnerable narcissists have a need to make themselves feel better about themselves and this is the reason why they tend to become sneaky and undermining. They may scrutinize your authority just to make create some trouble. When you understand that their behavior is originating from a place of uncertainty and insecurity, you can give them the necessary reassurance to ensure that they are working along with others and are focusing on the things that must be done A lot of reassurance and you'll fan their egocentric blazes, yet the perfect amount of reassurance will enable them to quiet down and get to the job that needs to be done.

Evaluating the context

Narcissism isn't an all-or-nothing sort of mentality. A few circumstances may evoke an individual's insecurities more than others. Suppose a lady was turned down for a promotion that she desired and now, she must keep working for an individual who indeed got the promotion she was vying for. With time, her insecurity is bound to worsen, and it will certainly make her more defensive, narcissistic, spiteful and even vindictive. If you are dealing with someone like this, then please keep in mind that the circumstances were responsible for the creation of the monster that you are left to deal with.

A positive outlook

In the event that you are managing narcissists who get joy from watching others suffer, at that point seeing the torment they cause will just egg them on to up their game. Try not to look unsettled, regardless of whether you're feeling irritated, and in the long run that conduct will lessen in recurrence. Besides, by remembering the past tips, you might most likely be able to help ease the situation and this will certainly improve the situation.

Don't get derailed

Try not to give yourself a chance to get derailed. It's rather easy to lose your very own feeling of direction or objectives when a narcissist tries to take the center stage in life. You don't have to do or follow everything this individual says or does, regardless of how much he clamors for your attention. You must find the harmony between advancing toward your goal and reducing the anxieties and insecurities of the vulnerable narcissist. If it happens to be a grandiose sort of narcissist, it might be a good idea to merely acknowledge his feelings so that you can move on.

Sense of humor

Keep your humor and don't let go of it. Challenging a

narcissist's bluff may imply that you overlook the person, yet it may also imply that you call their bluff and laugh it off. Without being mean about it, you can point to the inappropriateness of the individual's egocentric conduct with a grin or even a joke. This would be especially proper for the grandiose kind of narcissist, who will likely think that it's engaging and entertaining.

The person might need help

Since certain narcissists really have low confidence and significant sentiments of inadequacy, it's essential to perceive when they need professional help. Regardless of the belief that narcissism is immutable, it can be managed with the right therapy. So, keep all these simple things in mind while you are dealing with a narcissist.

Victim of Narcissistic Abuse

Envision this - your whole reality has been twisted and misshapen. You have been brutally abused, controlled, deceived, mocked, disparaged and gas lighted into trusting that you are imagining things. The individual you thought you knew and the life you built together has been broken into thousands of little fragments. Your sense of self has been disintegrated and reduced. You were first admired, then depreciated and at that point, you were pushed off the pedestal the narcissist placed you on. Maybe you were even displaced and replaced on various occasions, just to be 'hoovered' and attracted once again into the cycle of maltreatment that became worse than ever. Possibly you were tirelessly stalked, harassed and tormented to remain with the narcissistic abuser.

This was no ordinary separation or relationship; this was a

set-up for clandestine and tricky murder of your psyche and feeling of wellbeing. However, there may not be obvious scars to tell the story; all that you are now left with are broken pieces.

This stuff sounds like it came right out of a psychological thriller. Well, this is what narcissistic maltreatment or abuse looks like.

Mental savagery violence by threatening narcissists can incorporate verbal and psychological mistreatment, dangerous projection, stonewalling, damage, smear crusades, triangulation alongside plenty of different types of coercion and control. This is forced by somebody who needs sympathy, displays an extensive sense of entitlement and constantly tries to exploit others to meet their own needs.

Because of incessant maltreatment, the unfortunate casualties of narcissistic abuse may battle with side effects of PTSD and Complex PTSD if they had extra injuries that were doled out by narcissistic parents. Apart from all this, they might also suffer from what is known as "Narcissistic Victim Syndrome." The consequence of narcissistic abuse can incorporate misery, uneasiness, hyper vigilance, an inescapable feeling of lethal disgrace, emotional flashbacks that relapse the abused individual back to the abusive episodes, and overpowering feelings of powerlessness and uselessness.

When we are amidst a progressing abuse cycle, it very well may be hard to pinpoint precisely what we are encountering in light of the fact that abusers can twist the reality to suit their needs and use different forms of manipulation to convince their victims that they aren't victims and it's all in their head. If you notice that you are experiencing any of the different symptoms discussed in this section, then you are either or might have been in a toxic relationship with a narcissistic abuser.

You experience separation as a means of survival

You feel emotionally and physically detached from all that's around you and might experience the distortion of your memory, perception, the perception of self as well as that of your consciousness. As Dr. Van der Kolk (2015) writes in his book, The Body Keeps the Score, Dissociation is the essence of trauma. The overwhelming experience is split off and fragmented so that the emotions, sounds, images, thoughts and physical sensations take on a life of their own."

Separation or disassociation can euthanize or desensitize the emotions of an individual even when the said individual lived through horrendous conditions. Mind-desensitizing exercises, fixations, addictions and constraint may turn into a lifestyle since they give you the means to escape from your present reality. Your mind discovers approaches to sincerely shut out the effect of your torment, so you don't have to deal with all the pain that will come flooding back when you are no longer desensitized.

You may likewise create traumatized 'inward parts' that become disjointed from the identity you assume with your abuser or friends and family. These inward parts can include the parts of your inner child that was not nurtured, the annoyance and the sickening emotions you feel towards your abuser or the parts of yourself that you believe you can't express around them.

As per specialist Rev. Sheri Heller says, "Integrating and

reclaiming dissociated and disowned aspects of the personality is largely dependent on constructing a cohesive narrative, which allows for the assimilation of emotional, cognitive, and physiological realities." The best way to work on his internal healing is by seeking the services of a psychologist or a therapist.

You tread lightly

A typical side effect of abuse is abstaining from whatever that reminds you of the trauma you suffered- regardless of whether it refers to individuals, places or activities that represent the abuse. Regardless of whether it is your companion, your friend, your relative, colleague or supervisor, you tend to watch what you say or do around this person lest he unleashes his wrath on you, and you become an object that he must discipline.

In any case, you find this does not work and you are still the abuser's target. the abuser will still use you as an emotional punching bag whenever he feels like it. All this tends to make you anxious all the time about 'inciting' your abuser in any capacity and may stay away from avoiding any confrontation or setting of boundaries. You might expand this behavior of pleasing others to your outside world and will end up walking on eggshells all the time. you get used to treading lightly to prevent upsetting your abuser.

Giving up control

You set aside your essential needs and wants, relinquishing your enthusiastic and even your physical security to satisfy the abuser. You may have once been brimming with life, objective driven and dream-oriented. Presently you feel as though you are living just to satisfy the necessities and plans of someone else. Once, the narcissist's whole life appeared to rotate around you; presently your whole life spins around them. You may have put your objectives, interests, relationships as well as your personal wellbeing as a second thought just to guarantee that your abuser feels 'fulfilled' in the relationship. You will soon realize that the abuser will never pay any real attention to your needs or necessities.

Realize

You are battling with medical problems and substantial side effects that speak to your mental issues. You may have gained or lost a lot of weight, created genuine health problems that did not exist earlier and experienced physical side effects of premature aging. The worry of ceaseless maltreatment has sent your cortisol levels into overdrive and your immune system has been compromised. You find that you aren't able to sleep and keep on reliving the trauma over and over again.

You build up an unavoidable feeling of mistrust

Now, each individual that you come across seems to represent a danger and you end up getting restless about the intentions of others, particularly after having encountered the pernicious activities of somebody you once trusted. Your usual level of concern moves toward becoming hyper vigilance. Since the narcissistic abuser has endeavored to gaslight you into trusting that all that you experience are invalid, you experience serious difficulties about confiding in anybody, including yourself.

You self-disconnect

Numerous abusers not only isolate their unsuspecting victims, but the victims seem to isolate themselves because they feel like they are ashamed of the abuse their experience. All the victim blaming mindsets coupled with misconceptions about emotional and mental abuse in the society might make the victims feel stigmatized and their trauma doubles. They dread nobody will comprehend or trust them, so as opposed to connecting for help, they choose to pull back from others as an approach to keep away from judgment and countering from their abuser.

Those who are traumatized may at times compare themselves with others in more joyful and happy relationships or end up asking why their abuser seems to treat total outsiders with more regard. This can send them down the rabbit hole of wondering- "Why me?" All this just makes the victim get stuck in an endless tunnel of self-blame. The reality is that the only person to be blamed is the abuser and no one else. So, if you feel like you are stuck in an abusive relationship, then understand that you aren't to be blamed and that you must do everything you can to remove yourself from the abusive relationship.

Self-damage and self-destruct

Victims regularly end up reflecting over the maltreatment that was doled out to them and keep hearing the abuser's voice in their psyches. All this intensifies any negative self-talk that might have been going on in their heads and this propels them towards self-damage. Malignant narcissists 'program' and condition their victims to self-destruct- at times even to the point of forcing them to suicide.

Because of the narcissist's clandestine and clear put-downs, verbal maltreatment and hypercriticism, victims start developing the trait of rebuffing themselves since they convey such toxic shame. They may sabotage their objectives, dreams and scholastic interests. The abuser has ingrained in them a feeling of uselessness and they start to trust that they are undeserving of anything that's good.

You dread doing what you cherish and making progress.

Since numerous obsessive predators are envious of their oblivious victims, they rebuff them for succeeding. This conditions their victims from associating all things that they enjoy with the negative treatment that's conveniently doled out by the narcissist.

Chapter 4: Regain Control

Get Your Life Back on Track

A standout among the most troublesome things about overcoming narcissistic maltreatment is moving the dynamic from abiding in agony and ruminating on the past to developing the energy to push yourself toward a brighter and a happier future. Pain is obviously the natural response to any form of abuse; it might have made you quite upset and might have also annihilated any feelings of self you had. So, it is okay to accept the fact that you are dealing with a lot.

The intellectual discord of these two conflicting ideas—one being the narcissist as your perfect partner, and the other that of your ex as a merciless manipulator—is at the base of all the perplexity that you experience when the toxic relationship finally comes to an end. A lot of people who were victims of narcissistic abuse seem to spend a lot of their time wondering "how could he do that to me? I thought that he loved and adored me!"

Remember that narcissists, borderlines, sociopaths, psychopaths or any combination of all such people aren't individuals who go from being normal to their abusive self only in times of stress. Stress isn't a trigger for the change in their personality. You must understand that they suffer from a personality disorder and that it is called the same for a reason. It is as much a part of their lives as the need to breathe.

Most abusers and manipulators tend to project their distorted perceptions onto their unsuspecting victim! Your attributes of sympathy, empathy and pardoning run deep and make you question the intentions behind the narcissist's loathsome behavior. So, you give them the benefit of doubt- over and over again. You might be doing this out of love or compassion that you feel for the other person, but the other person will surely think of this as a means to push you further along. Rather than settling anything, your thoughtfulness combined the way their rationalizing of behavior ensures that the cycle of abuse doesn't stop.

So, you at last stir and wake up to the cruel truth and escape. That good, but now what? Now, it is time to heal yourself- emotionally and mentally. At first, it might seem like a steep climb where you keep slipping up after every step or two. It might also seem like you aren't making any progress. But remember that it merely seems this way and isn't true. Here are some tips that will come in handy while trying to heal yourself and getting your life back on track.

The best way to regain control of your life is by learning to be happy. In this section, you will learn about different things that you can do to concentrate on living a happy and fulfilling life while forgetting about all the nasty incidents of the past.

There are some days when you feel like there's rocket fuel pumping through your veins. Days when you feel like you can overcome everything and anything that life throws at you. However, there are a few days when it feels like everything is weighing down on you. Have you ever felt like this? Well, haven't we all? Happiness is a practice and it is up to us to learn it. Happiness is a daily choice and you get to train your mind to be happy. This doesn't mean that you must stay focused on your mood all the time. Whenever you feel your mood shifting, the tiniest bit of conscious effort can make all the difference. Life will constantly keep giving you lemons. It depends on you whether you want to make lemonade out of it. So, get ready. Here are a few things that you can do on a daily basis to improve your happiness quotient.

Start your day with a bang

As soon as you wake up, do something that will make the rest of the day a success for you. This is the trick that you need to get right. It is quite easy to roll out of bed, check your email, or watch some TV. This will just make your day meaningless. Doesn't it feel good when you have made some progress on something that's meaningful in your life? Then why don't you do something about it? The previous night, before sleeping, make a simple plan as to the first task that you need to tackle in the morning. It can be something as simple as working out for an hour. What is that one thing that will make your day a success? It can be anything. If you know what it is, then get to it the minute you wake up in the morning.

You don't have to rush through your day. Rushing through things will not only make you stressed out, but it will also kill your happiness. Stop believing that you haven't got the time to enjoy the things around you. Take some time and smell the roses. There is always time and don't be under the misconception that you need to hurry up all the time. If you don't take some time out, the roses will die eventually. Plan to do maybe one or two important things daily. Don't fill up your entire calendar with tasks that you need to accomplish. Human beings tend to have ridiculous notions about what they can accomplish and how quickly they can get things done. Hence, at the end of the day, all that we are left with is stress and disappointment. So, why don't you try slowing down for a while? Walk slower, drive slowly and chew slowly. Relish everything you are doing.

If you feel rushed all the time, then you will never feel that you have the time to enjoy the small wonders of the world you live in. Do little things like walking barefoot in the sand, playing with a dog, going for a stroll with no destination in mind, watching the sunrise or the sunset, or just take a minute to appreciate the world around you. You will truly feel amazed by the difference that slowing down can make.

Get lost in happiness

Take a few minutes and think about all those bits of your life that you are grateful for. It can be something big or small. Things that you are proud of, the things that make you smile, and the things you enjoy; the people who mean a lot to you, and those whom you are grateful to have around yourself. You can do this anywhere you are. You can do this while at work, while working out, or even while traveling. When you start feeling sheer gratitude, it is not possible to feel any form of negative emotions like stress or anger.

We all must have things that make us instantly happy. The things that make you smile, inspire you, or simply make you happy. It can be a movie, a song, a video, a specific book, or even a friend. Make sure that you keep a track of these things. Spend a few minutes and make this list. Keep adding on things whenever you notice that something puts a smile on your face. The next time you are feeling low, just refer to this list.

This is the simplest and the most powerful thing ever. It is as contagious as it gets. Keep smiling. Strive to be known as the person who is always smiling. If you see someone frowning, smile at them. Smile the biggest smile you possibly can. All it takes is a few people to reciprocate the same and after this, it will just keep on spreading. Also, studies show that smiling creates a chemical reaction in the brain that makes us happy.

When you are feeling low, the last thing you will want to do is be around other people. Resist doing this at any cost. Life is about forming relationships and connections. The ones you love can change your mood in an instant. Make sure that you choose people carefully. You need people who are positive and who will bring positivity into your life. Anyone who doesn't fit this bill is certainly not worth your while. Stay away from negative people and all forms of negativity.

Being selfless can make you happy too. Do something good for someone else. This is bound to make you feel better about yourself. It can be something as simple as just holding the door open for someone or letting someone else get ahead of you in the queue. It doesn't have to be anything extravagant. The smallest of deeds can make you feel happy.

Now you know the routine that you can make use of for being happy

Happiness is a basic human motivation. However, only one out of three people can say that they are happy. How often have you complained about having to wait in a queue at the airport for boarding your flight or crib about wasting time when your flight got delayed? We keep hearing complaints about these things or you might have complained about it too. It's like we have forgotten that it's incredible that human beings can fly! How can we be so quick to take all these wonderful things that happen in our lives for granted?

Why is it so easy for us to complain? Why do we tend to focus on all things negative? However, you can achieve happiness even without all the wonderful technology in the world. Instead of being reactive to the things that are happening around them, happy people are the ones that take control of their lives and their emotions. If you are not happy with yourself, then you have no one to blame other than yourself. Also, will it make your life any better if you can blame someone else or something else? Bad things keep happening to everyone. Life isn't about what happens, it is about the manner in which you respond to it. Here are the ten behaviors that can help to change your life and make you a happy person.

Not everything in your life will go exactly in the manner that you have planned. There will be setbacks. Things happen. We might mess things up. Obsessing too much over things and making your happiness dependent on outcomes will do you no good whatsoever. You will need to learn to be happy, come what may. We tend to get in our own way. We do this without releasing it. You will need to quit worrying about a specific outcome. Things will happen and there will be things that are beyond your control. The only thing you can control is your actions. You cannot control the situations you are in. You must stop worrying about obtaining a specific result. Instead, concentrate on the manner in which you can make most of what's given to you. If you try too hard to get a certain result, you will tend to get in your own way. Desperation will not get you the results you want. It will just hinder your growth. Stop trying to fit in where you don't belong. If the shoe doesn't fit, it is time to move on. Find something that you are comfortable in.

No two humans are alike. So, why must we all have just one

standard for measuring success? All of us end up getting stuck in the rat race that the society has created towards achieving the so-called standard of "success" that are set by society. There will always be someone that's better than you at something or the other. There will never be sufficient time to do everything. Instead, you must focus on the things you opt for. When you select something, you have simultaneously rejected something else. This is the norm of life and it is perfectly all right to do so. It is quite wonderful, how we get to choose what we want. You will need to define what happiness, success, and wealth mean to you. You cannot let society decide what you need or think you need. If that's the case, then you will always fall short of something or the other. You will need to stop comparing yourself to others and stop competing with others. This is the only manner in which you will get ahead in life. Pull yourself out of the endless rat race and the rut you are stuck in.

How many times have you told yourself "just this once?" Most of us have convinced ourselves that we are capable of breaking our own rules. We will always find reasons to justify these small choices we make. None of these things really feel like a major decision initially. However, over a period of time, these things end up forming a part of the bigger picture. Human beings are good at sabotaging their own selves. People tend to behave in a manner that goes against their goals or ideals. The gap between what you do and what you must be doing must be as small as possible. The smaller this gap is the happier you will be in life. Giving 100% commitment is easier than giving 98%. When you have committed yourself fully to something, then this means that the decision has already been made. Unless and until you are fully committed to something, you will always end up being a victim of all the external circumstances in life. If you simply rely on your willpower, it is more likely that you will end up crumbling. You might think that you are doing better than what you actually are doing. You needn't rely on your willpower once you have given your 100% commitment. Regardless of the circumstances, your decision has been made. It is all about being proactive instead of being reactive.

Abundance and the lack of it tend to exist simultaneously in our life. It is always our choice which of these things we tend to. When you have decided to focus your energy on what you have in your life instead of focusing on things that are missing. Happiness is a very simple concept. It can be as simple as gratitude that you feel. According to research, there are certain physical, psychological, and social benefits of feeling gratitude. These benefits include a stronger immune system, reduction in body aches and pains, better blood pressure, and better sleep too. The psychological benefits are increased feelings of positivity, you'll feel more alert, experience more joy, and be optimistic. The social benefits are that you will feel more helpful, generous, compassionate, forgiving, outgoing, and less isolated. In spite of all these benefits, most people are usually ungrateful. People tend to focus too much of their time and attention on what they don't have. The grass always does seem greener on the other side. If it were one thing that you want, after achieving it, it will be something else. There is no end to this ever-growing list of wants. Life has become a constant race of having the best of things. How can you ever be happy when all you want from life is more things? Take a moment and appreciate what you have.

Human beings, in general, need to learn to be more grateful.

Your happiness depends on your ability to be grateful. Here are a few things that you can do to be more grateful in life. You must maintain a gratitude journal. Fill this up with instances of moments of sincere gratitude associated with the most commonplace events that take place. This will help you in making you more grateful. Think about all the challenges that you have overcome in life. This will help you in being grateful for what you have in life. You cannot truly embrace what you have in life if you don't remember the struggle you had to go through to get what you have. Here are a few questions that you can ask yourself that'll help you with self-introspection. Ask yourself, what you have received from, given to, and the troubles you have caused. These questions will help to give your life some perspective and you will start looking at things from a different perspective. You can learn a few prayers of gratitude as well. In most of the cultures and spiritual traditions that exist, there are prayers of gratitude. Such prayers are considered to be the most powerful of all. It allows an individual to connect with divine power. Lack of awareness and forgetfulness are the two main causes of impeding gratitude. You can make use of visual reminders that will help trigger thoughts of gratitude. You need to literally come to your senses. You will need to be more present in what you see, touch, smell, hear, taste and feel. The feeling of gratitude will intensify when you are more present in the moment.

Be conscious of the language that you use. People who are grateful make use of different words like gifts, abundance, blessings, fortune, fortunate, and blessed more frequently. If you start incorporating these words into your daily vocabulary, you will realize that the list of things that you need to be grateful for continues to increase. This will allow you to realize and appreciate the abundance that is present all around you. Smile a lot and say thank you when someone does something for you. It can be something as simple as thanking someone for holding the door open for you.

Start saying, "I Love You" more often. This might sound really strange. Try saying, "I love you" to your friends and family members. They will all be pleasantly surprised. However, make sure that you are being sincere while saying this. Saying these three simple words will not only change the person to whom you have said this, but it will change you as well. Simply by saying these words, you will feel more love towards that person. It is important for others to know that they are valued and cherished. If you love someone, tell them so. Everything is transient in life, who knows when you will get the next opportunity to tell them that you love them? You will get immense satisfaction by making others happy. You get what you give. You give others positivity and you will get positivity in turn.

Most of us have hobbies; however, these hobbies are just that, hobbies. This is perfectly okay. We all need something that helps us to forget about reality for a while. However, research has shown that an individual is capable of experiencing leisure while doing anything. Even your work can become a leisurely activity for you. Leisure is something that rejuvenates you. When you have decided the direction in which you want your life to head in, then you can consciously choose your hobbies. Choose such hobbies that will get you to where your goal is. Your hobbies will not only help to provide you with some relaxation, but they will also push you towards your goals.

You needn't wait until tomorrow for something that you can do today itself. Happiness is all about embracing the present that we live in. it is about not letting that moment just pass you by. Never miss out on the important things in life for something that you think is "important." What you might think will impress someone might just be considered to be a flaw in your character. Get rid of all the things that are not essential or vital to your being. There is nothing in this life that can be considered to be permanent. Everything is transient. Children grow up, friends tend to move away, and our loved ones pass on to the other side. Always live in the present. Don't forget to appreciate what you have in life. Always take the time to appreciate the things you cherish, before it is too late.

You will need to step outside of your comfort zone if you want to grow in life. A happy person is comfortable outside their comfort zone. You will need to challenge yourself in order to grow. Growth is a major prerequisite for happiness. If you aren't growing and improving, then you are becoming stagnant and are decaying. Taking a risk will make you feel alive and it will put you in a state of consciousness that will enable you to perform to the best of your ability. You will become thoroughly engaged in what you are doing. When you are doing things that are outside your comfort zone, then you will improve your conscious level as well. The probability of failure will force you to think better and different from your usual routine. Your mind will be forced to get creative and innovative. Sadly, most people tend to play safely in life. Their goals are usually logical. There is little or no element of risk that is involved. You must take risks in life. Do those things that make you feel alive. Activate the energy within you. Of course, when there are risks involved there will be failures too. Don't think of a failure as the end. It is just a temporary setback and it can be easily overcome. There is no need to give up. Experience the good and the bad in life. This is the only way in which you will grow. Promise yourself that you will do all those things that scare you. Take them one at a time.

Most of the time, people end up spending their time on things that are urgent even though they are unimportant. We wake up in the morning, and the first thing that we do is check our messages or emails. We have programmed ourselves to be reactive instead of being proactive. A happy person will always make important things a priority. Not just important, but important and non-urgent things as well. The things you must focus on will be exercising, reading meaningful books, setting goals for yourself, writing a journal, and spending time with your loved ones. None of the above-mentioned things are urgent. However, these things are very important. These things can be easily put on hold until the next day and they usually get postponed. The happy and successful people in the world tend to spend most of their time on the things that are important. One way in which you can do this will be by waking up early in the morning. Establish a morning routine for yourself. You can meditate or exercise, go for a jog, play with your pet, or do something that you enjoy. This will make you feel positive about the rest of the day and keep you motivated as well.

Forgoing the good for pursuing the best. There are a lot of things in life that are good, and even great. This doesn't mean that you must do them all. Every day, you are faced with once in lifetime opportunities. Most people tend to grab onto any great opportunity that comes their way, even though it is not in synchronization with their vision in life. This is the reason why the lives of people tend to move in different directions. They can't move in a single direction on a conscious level. On the contrary, a happy person will refuse the most amazing opportunity as well. They will not want to sacrifice their freedom for the sake of security. They will not let distractions divert their attention. There are only select things in life that can be described as the very "best." You are the only one that gets to decide what's best for you. Don't keep yourself occupied with the so-called "good" activities and miss out on the amazing ones.

Happy people are the ones that live in the present. They don't let go of those moments that matter. They are always grateful for what they have. Happy people focus on those aspects of their life that are significant.

Do you want to be able to manage your stress in a better manner? Get rid of all the bad memories and want to simply feel happier? Then there are a few exercises that you can make use of for boosting your happiness. Try these exercises for a week and you will notice a positive change in your behavior.

One door shuts and the other open. Take into consideration any negative moment in your life that has led you towards a positive outcome; an outcome that you weren't expecting. Make a note of these things every day.

Time is precious. Spending time with someone is the best gift you can possibly give them. So, this week you will need to offer the gift of "time" to three different people. This can be in the form of helping them around the house, taking a person who's feeling lonely out for a meal, or even catching up with an old friend. These things must be done in addition to your other planned activities.

Keep a journal wherein you can write down the kind deeds

you performed in a day. Make a note in your journal before going to bed at night.

Every day, you should write about the three funny things that you experienced throughout the day. Also, make a note of the cause of the occurrence of such a funny incident. Was it something you said, observed, or was it something spontaneous?

Think of someone who has had a positive impact on your life and write a letter of gratitude to that person. If it is possible, you can also deliver it to them in person.

The good things: Write about the three good things that you got to experience in a day. Also, state the reasons why such things had occurred.

If you aren't keen on writing things down, then in such a case you must consider discussing the same with someone who is close to you. Talk to yourself about all the positive aspects of your life. Also, make sure that you have practiced the above-mentioned steps for at least one full week.

Stop an Argument with A Narcissist

Here are the means you should take

Try not to contend about 'right' and 'wrong'

There's no point attempting to make sense of who is "to be faulted" for something, as narcissists will never concede blame. They need to reprimand you for any negative feelings they are feeling since they absolutely depend on the picture they are depicting as being impeccable.

Rather, attempt to understand their emotions

In the event that you are with a narcissist, in any case, you likely as of now have a ton of compassion. In any case, even the most minding individuals battle to see the feeling of having it for somebody who is flinging a great many insults at them.

In any case, on the off chance that you end up getting into a tight spot, one approach to sooth a narcissist's fury is to relate to their sentiments, and state something like: "You probably felt extremely harmed by what I did, I can comprehend why you are feeling that way."

Use 'we' language

By saying "we" instead of "I" or "you," you incorporate yourself in the conduct. The narcissist is likely so irate at you since you set out to guard yourself, so to attempt and stop the contention raising further you can attempt and remind them you're in this together, and it'll be in an ideal situation for everybody to stop.

Try not to anticipate an expression of remorse

There's no possibility of the narcissist admitting to any bad behavior or saying 'sorry' This incorporates requesting that they process what truly transpired. A narcissist will not be fine with the possibility that they were the ones who started an argument over something, especially if the matter in question is quite trivial. So, it is better to just move on instead of holding your breath for an apology.

Get some information about a point that intrigues them

Narcissists love discussing themselves or talking about

things that they find interesting or care about them. This is quite similar to distracting a child by dangling a set of shiny keys in front of them. This causes the child to lose focus and in the same manner, you can use certain tactics to distract a narcissist. Don't attempt to do this during an ongoing argument, but you can certainly attempt this after the argument comes to an end.

Another thing that you can do is to request counsel. This may resemble a somewhat less straightforward method for changing the subject since it'll make the narcissist feel like they are the main individual you can go to and make them feel unrivaled.

Try not to take the lure yourself

As the narcissist trusts you have harmed them seriously by whatever they figure you did, they'll need to do likewise to you. This implies they'll toss everything at you, from that one time you got into a fight a year earlier, to how you're acting childishly at this moment.

Essentially, they are attempting to get the most extreme reaction out of you they can. By overlooking the insult or the dig the narcissist takes at you, you can easily avoid an unnecessary fight. In the event that you take the bait, things are probably going to go out of control, and you're viable giving the narcissist precisely what they need - your agony.

Make sure to put yourself first

Most specialists think being in a sentimental relationship or any emotional relationship with a narcissist is a candidly depleting, harming the process. At last, it's up to you on the off chance that you think the dreary inner self-stroking and diligent work is justified, despite all the trouble or not.

No doubt, you'll most likely acknowledge it isn't, and you'll one day have the capacity to proceed onward with your existence without the narcissist keeping you down. In any case, meanwhile, utilizing these strategies to de-heighten a narcissist who is having some fantastic luck can help get you out of irritating, and possibly perilous, circumstances.

Overcome Narcissistic Tendencies

Have you at any point been informed that you can be absolutely self-absorbed most of the time? Do individuals resent your extraordinary fearlessness? Or on the other hand, maybe you've even been informed that you have to figure out how to quit being a narcissist.

You may feel that the world is against you- essentially in light of the fact that you like to put yourself over the rest. While the facts confirm that self-esteem can be solid for us now and again, as the familiar saying goes, a lot of something can end up destructive and unsafe.

You may basically need the best for yourself, however organizing yourself at the expense of other individuals' sentiments is an indication of narrow-mindedness and an absence of sympathy.

Will narcissists be able to change?

Conceding one's deficiencies is never simple—particularly for a narcissist. However, on the off chance that you are perusing this, you've likely officially recognized the results of such conduct. Maybe you are inspired to figure out how to quit being a narcissist and to at last alter your way of living.

Individuals will, in general, say that it is inconceivable for narcissists to change. Be that as it may, truly, it's never past the point where it is possible to start from the very beginning again and to remake connections—insofar as there is a realistic aim.

Here are some ways in which you can do this.

Stage one - acknowledge the roots of narcissism

Numerous individuals befuddle self-centeredness and vanity with narcissism—however, how can you distinguish between the two? One approach to distinguish narcissism is through their absolute lack of empathy or even sympathy for that matter.

Narcissists are less inclined to feel for the general population around them. It isn't sufficient for the spotlight to be on them—they additionally demonstrate no regret while slighting the sentiments of others. Narcissists are headed to win, regardless of the stuff. In the meantime, they don't trust that they are imperfect—all they see when they see themselves is flawlessness. This makes it hard to concede that change is required. The way to stop being a narcissist is to initially recognize the foundations of narcissism, and after that to rehearse sympathy and acknowledgment.

By understanding the significance of this absolute initial step, it will be simpler to continue with the other steps that are discussed in this section.

Stage two - be willing to hear other people out

This subsequent stage is presumably a standout amongst

the most troublesome difficulties a narcissist can ever confront- to listen and accept the opinion of others.

Narcissists hold a conviction that there is nothing amiss with them; that they are, truth be told, impeccable. They will in general trust that the world needs to make up for lost time to their unimaginably exclusive requirements and in this manner, nobody is by all accounts worth their time.

Set aside the effort to truly tune in to the voices of others. You probably won't care for what they are stating, however, this training really encourages you to remain grounded and associated. Narcissists are accustomed to seeing themselves high over the positions, which abandons them disconnected to their environment.

Stage three - put yourself in others' shoes

Compassion has never been in the vocabulary of a narcissist. Furthermore, the pitiful part is, compassion isn't something that can be gained from a course of reading. Understanding the feelings and circumstances of others must be finished by placing ourselves in their place. Even though it is difficult to truly understand what others might feel, essentially envisioning how we may respond to such circumstances is a decent spot to begin.

It is extremely simple to wind up apathetic regarding circumstances and feelings that don't have any significant bearing to us. Because we can't feel similar feelings, it doesn't imply that they are insignificant, particularly when we are the reason for another's affliction.

When we enable ourselves to feel what others may feel, we figure out how to be progressively dependable toward the welfare of others.

Stage four - be mindful of your own actions

Narcissists are typically blamed for being self-obsessed and this is why they are often called out for their excessive vanity. As of not long ago, you may have just been worried about your mental self-image. You might detest committing errors, particularly before others. Be that as it may, you may additionally love to rub your accomplishments in other individuals' shortcomings.

Take a moment, stop doing all this and look at the master plan, you will understand that this conduct is an indication of low confidence. While a narcissist may feel moment satisfaction by being the best, their requirement for consideration and acknowledgment is their very shortcoming. To turn into the safe and substance individual that you truly are, you have to focus on how you carry on.

Each time you have the desire to discuss yourself, get some information about their day. You'll be amazed at the outcomes—focus on them, and they'll be all the more eager to hear you out as well.

Stage five - give yourself time to heal

You can't change something that has been continuing for a considerable length of time. Figuring out how to quit being a narcissist will take a great deal of time. Beside pushing forward, accept this as an open door to lament too. Ponder, unwind, and think about those minutes.

It is said that narcissists become their identity due to their environment. This is particularly valid for the individuals who experienced childhood in an unsupportive family unit, or maybe an awful accident in your past formed you into the individual you are today. Utilize this opportunity to enable yourself to feel those agonies, and after that let them go.

You may likewise be lamenting about broken relationships and lost chances all due to your narcissistic ways. Allow yourself to mend rather than continually battling back- quit reprimanding others the way you feel and to begin being in charge of your own feelings. All things considered, it's you that chooses how you respond to things.

Rather than retaliating, or continually looking for an approach to settle the score, enable yourself to end up helpless. Trust it or not, there is quality in appearing. Since you know the torment, you will be progressively watchful in managing other individuals' sentiments too.

Stage six - don't wait for or expect praise

If you have gone this far, give yourself a merited congratulatory gesture- however, don't anticipate that other individuals should do likewise.

Narcissists are constantly eager for recognition. It is the thing that drives them forward and makes them transform everything into a challenge. There's nothing amiss with needing to get a compliment or two. In any case, when it turns into the ultimate objective, everything else loses its importance. Narcissists regularly trust that they are qualified for applause and compliments. Truth be told, they don't just need other individuals' consideration; they additionally need their affirmation.

Understand that praise isn't something that should fuel

your confidence. The void you may feel does not originate from an absence of compliments—it is presumably on the grounds that your accomplishment has lost its significance as of now.

Try not to accomplish something for them to attain the approval of others. Do it just on the grounds that you cherish doing it, and because accomplishing your objective issues most to you. In a similar light, very few individuals will give you a series of praise just on the grounds that you've figured out how to quit being a narcissist. All things considered; it is your very own business.

What's more, recall, while you may do this to refute others, you'll discover more significance in this in case you're doing it for yourself first.

Stage seven - practice kindness

Practicing kindness is simpler than you might suspect. At a more critical look, there are numerous open doors in our regular daily existences where we can demonstrate benevolence to the general population in our locale.

Welcome your neighbor with a major grin as you head out to work. Compliment your associate on their marvelous OOTD (outfit of the day). Indeed, even a basic thank you to the barista who readies your espresso perfectly consistently indicates generosity.

The motivation behind why narcissists may think that it's difficult to be decent to others is that they see things from a conceited perspective.

They probably won't welcome their neighbors since they believe them to be all out, outsiders. They don't compliment their associates on the grounds that their very own outfits are way better in any case. What's more, they don't state thank you to their barista in light of the fact that they paid for the administration.

Rehearsing consideration hones our aptitude of being careful toward others. We are tested to consider the prosperity of others before our own. Rather than concentrating on yourself first, individuals who practice consideration consistently ask how they can help.

This training likewise removes us from childishness—a propensity narcissists are constantly blamed for.

All in all, what are you sitting tight for? Show somebody a little graciousness today and you'll be amazed at how appreciative they will be for your quality.

Stage eight - be content

Narcissists have terrible notoriety of being jealous. They simply loathe seeing other individuals' content with something they don't have and may even attempt to dependably exceed the accomplishments of the general population around them.

They one-up another person's activity with a discussion about their advancement. When another person returns from an away trek, they abruptly talk about their up and coming Caribbean journey.

To put it plainly, whatever other individuals have, they have something better.

Is it true that it isn't exceptionally tiring to see the world as a challenge rather than basically being cheerful for other people?

When we don't have the foggiest idea of how to celebrate in the bliss of others, we can't anticipate that they should cheer for us. Odds are, they couldn't think less about what you have- particularly when you make it seem like you have everything on the planet.

Rather than endeavoring to rival everyone, find a sense of contentment with yourself and figure out how to be content with what you have. Regularly, we are so caught up with pursuing new, "better" things, which we overlook the estimation of what we as of now have.

Love your life and rejoice it. Celebrate life. Be grateful for what you have. Don't give up easily. Congratulate yourself on every hurdle that you have overcome. Don't let negativity get to you. By following these simple suggestions, you can start loving your life.

Learn to be grateful and practice gratitude. Instead of thinking that you don't have something, learn to be thankful for what you have. This doesn't mean that you stop being ambitious. Stop trying to please others and be who you are. Learn to live in the present. Let the past be a learning experience, but don't let it hold you back. Think about your future, but don't let it overshadow your present. Acknowledge your accomplishments and be proud of all that you have accomplished. Small or big, always celebrate your accomplishments. Show your loved ones that they are loved and stay true to yourself.

Conclusion

I want to thank you once again for purchasing this book. I hope this book proved to be an entertaining and engaging read.

By now you might have obviously realized that narcissists are everywhere, and we all tend to deal with them in some aspect of our lives, one way or another. If you don't want a narcissist to dictate your life, then you must learn to deal with them. There are different things that you can do to sever the ties with a narcissist, regain control of your life and get your life back on track. Apart from this, you were also provided information about the ways in which you can recognize a narcissist and the ways in which you can prevent someone from turning into a narcissist. Now, all that's left is for you to start taking action to deal with the narcissist in your life.

Thank you and I wish you all the best!

References

14 Signs You're Dealing With A Narcissist. (2019). Retrieved from https://www.mindbodygreen.com/articles/14-signs-of-narcissism

6 Signs of Narcissism You May Not Know About. (2019). Retrieved from https://www.psychologytoday.com/us/blog/evolution-the-self/201311/6-signs-narcissism-you-may-not-know-about

Narcissistic Personality Disorder: Practice Essentials, Background, Pathophysiology and Etiology. (2019). Retrieved from https://emedicine.medscape.com/article/1519417-overview#a3

Narcissistic Personality Disorder Symptoms, Treatment & Causes. (2019). Retrieved from https://www.medicinenet.com/narcissistic_personality_disorder/article.htm#what_are_narcissistic_personality_disorder_symptoms_and_signs

What Is Healthy Narcissism?. (2019). Retrieved from https://www.psychologytoday.com/us/blog/contemporary-psychoanalysis-in-action/201609/what-is-healthy-narcissism

5 Types of Extreme Narcissists (and How to Deal With Them). (2019). Retrieved from https://www.psychologytoday.com/us/blog/shame/201509/5-types-extreme-narcissists-and-how-deal-them

5 Ways To Deal With A Narcissistic Parent. (2019).

Retrieved from https://thoughtcatalog.com/rebecca-coleman/2014/03/5-ways-to-deal-with-a-narcissistic-parent/

The Survival Guide for Living With a Narcissist. (2019). Retrieved from https://www.psychologytoday.com/us/blog/understanding-narcissism/201710/the-survival-guide-living-narcissist

10 Powerful Ways to Deal With Your Narcissistic Boss. (2019). Retrieved from https://www.inc.com/lolly-daskal/10-powerful-ways-to-deal-with-your-narcissistic-bo.html

Narcissism In Children: What Are The Signs And How To Deal With It?. (2019). Retrieved from https://www.momjunction.com/articles/unexpected-treatments-for-narcissistic-personality-disorder-in-your-kid_0083780/#gref

Narcissistic Injuries: What They Are and How to Protect Yourself from Them. (2019). Retrieved from https://psychcentral.com/lib/narcissistic-injuries-what-they-are-and-how-to-protect-yourself-from-them/

8 Ways to Handle a Narcissist. (2019). Retrieved from https://www.psychologytoday.com/us/blog/fulfillment-any-age/201408/8-ways-handle-narcissist

5 Fresh Ideas for Keeping Narcissists Out of Your Life. (2019). Retrieved from https://psychcentral.com/blog/5-fresh-ideas-for-keeping-narcissists-out-of-your-life/

10 Steps to Getting Your Life Back After Narcissistic Abuse. (2019). Retrieved from https://medium.com/@SoulGPS/10-steps-to-getting-

your-life-back-after-narcissistic-abuse-96b5c74af29c

The 8 Step Process On How To Stop Being A Narcissist - Learn Relaxation Techniques. (2019). Retrieved from https://learnrelaxationtechniques.com/how-to-stop-being-a-narcissist/

11 Signs You're the Victim of Narcissistic Abuse. (2019). Retrieved from https://blogs.psychcentral.com/recovering-narcissist/2017/08/11-signs-youre-the-victim-of-narcissistic-abuse/